How to Run a Successful Yoga Business and Not Go Broke

LESSONS FROM A YOGA TEACHER,
ENTREPRENEUR & MODERN HIPPIE

Michelle S. Fondin

Ordering Information: Quantity sales. Special discounts are available on quantity purchases by corporations, associations, and others. For details, contact author at michellefondinauthor@gmail.com

How to Run a Successful Yoga Business and Not Go Broke: Lessons from a Yoga Teacher, Entrepreneur, & Modern Hippie/ Michelle S. Fondin

Cover art and design by Jay Fondin. For logos and branding with Jay Fondin, email: jmfondin@gmail.com

ISBN 978-1976044199

Contents

Preface IX

Introduction 1

If I Knew Then What I Know Now 1

    Starting Out 3

    Spreading Myself Too Thin 4

    Running a Studio? 6

    Hitting the Erase Button & Going Back to Zero 7

Chapter One 11

Your Yoga Teacher Training Program 11

    Choosing the Right Teacher Training 11

    Reasons for Choosing a Program 12

    Elements of a Great Teacher Training Program 15

    Evaluating Training Courses 17

    Is Advanced Training Necessary? 18

Chapter Two 23

You Are Not a Monk, Unless You Are One 23

    Getting Into the Right Mindset 27

    Overcoming Poverty Consciousness 28

    Value Yourself & What You're Offering to Others 30

    Maximize Your Time & Give More 33

    Recap of Lessons Learned 34

    Your Yoga Business is Valuable 34

Chapter Three 36

Hey Dharma? What's Your Karma?..36

    Yoga Teaching Time...37

    Your Teaching Action Step List.................................39

    What Is Your X Factor?..42

    What Are Your Priorities in Life?...........................44

    Recap of Lessons Learned: Action Steps.................46

Chapter Four...48

Building a Reputation...48

    Create Your Personality...48

    Keep It Professional...49

    The No-Nos of Rapport...51

    Customer Service Nightmares...................................55

    Be Extraordinary..59

    Building Yourself Back Up When You're Down.............60

    Recap of Lessons Learned: Reputation.....................62

Chapter Five..65

Marketing Your Way to Success...65

    Your Target Market..66

    What Does Your Target Market Want?...........................67

    How to Reach Your Target Market............................69

    Must-Have Marketing..70

    Free Marketing...80

    Paid Marketing...89

    Recap on Lessons Learned: Marketing.....................94

Chapter Six..97

Your Business Model 97

    Your Legal Status 97

    Modeling: Learning from Successful Yoga Businesses Around You 102

    Your Business Philosophy 104

    Your Business Plan 105

    Who Will Help? 106

    Your Services and Products 108

    The Power of Focus 109

    Start Small & Keep It Simple 110

    Recap of Lessons Learned: Your Business Model 113

Chapter Seven 116

Financial Intelligence 116

    Start Up Funds 116

    Budget 120

    Cash Flow 121

    Tax Deductible Items 124

    Filing Taxes 127

    Know what's going on in your finances 129

    Recap of Lessons Learned: Finances 129

Chapter Eight 132

Opening & Running a Successful Yoga Studio 132

    Step One: Choose Your Business Partner 133

    Step Two: Choosing Your Studio Space 136

    Step Three: Hiring 140

Step Four: Plan Your Business Launch 145

Step Five: Plan for Growth 146

Recap of Lessons Learned: Opening a Studio...............148

Chapter Nine 151

Balancing Work & The Rest of Your Life..............................151

You Can't Give Away What You Don't Have................152

You Are Never a Guru in Your Own Home 153

Michelle's Top Ten for Living a Balanced Life.............155

Recap of Lessons Learned: Balancing Your Life 161

Epilogue..162

Appendix: Ideas for Places to Teach Yoga 164

Books and Products 165

Check out Michelle's other books....................................165

Index 166

Dedication

To my beautiful children, Jay, Mathieu, and Xavier. Thank you for being accepting of all the years I spent building a yoga business. We made a great team and I couldn't have done it without your support. You three are the best kids a mom could ask for and I'm so grateful to you and proud of the teens and adults you have become.

Love, Mom

Preface

THE DISCLAIMER ON THE pamphlet read something like this, *This yoga teacher training is not intended to be used for a new career or to replace your current salary. Most people who complete the training use it for supplemental income.* Something rebellious welled up inside of me. "I'll show them. I will use my yoga and Ayurveda training to build a business and an extraordinary income." Famous last words...

That's the way I tend to operate. Tell me I can't do something and I will do everything I can to prove you wrong. Tenacity is wonderful when it's channeled in the right direction. But stubbornness and over idealism can cause you to make horrible mistakes, so I've learned.

As the saying goes, *Hindsight is 20/20.* After nine years of experience, getting one breath away from bankruptcy, and living the devastation of not taking sound advice, I have come to understand the disclaimer on that brochure. If you're a newly trained yoga teacher or launching your own yoga studio, you may be wondering if you can make a decent living. Part of my assumption was correct; you can make a decent living by being a yoga teacher, but only by overcoming extreme challenges.

Many of us, who embark on this spiritual path, are not business savvy. Those who experience instant success, tend to already have a business background. However, this business is a unique animal. The people, who tend to train to teach yoga, aren't doing it to get rich. In fact, I've found, in talking with newly trained teachers over the years, that it's quite the opposite. In fact, many feel bad asking for money to give the experience to someone in need. In addition, in recent years, the market has become oversaturated with yoga teachers and yoga class offerings. So not only do you have to overcome the personal side, of creating a business out of a passion or spiritual mission, but also, you need to figure out how to stand apart from a New York City-sized crowd.

For those reasons and many more, creating a successful yoga business is one of the most challenging things I have ever endured. In this book, I will show you what to do in order to create a successful yoga business and most importantly what not to do. By following the advice in this book, you will not only avoid the many thousand dollar mistakes I made, but also save time, energy, and stay healthy. In the end, you will come out ahead of your peers. I'm writing this to you as a best friend talking over coffee. All of the advice I'm giving you is based on real experience and a heartfelt desire to see you succeed. So get your coffee or tea, grab a notebook and pen, and let's get started.

If I Knew Then What I Know Now

I'M AFFLICTED WITH WHAT some people might call the entrepreneurial spirit. Entrepreneurs aren't always the wisest in the bunch. They might be the most enthusiastic, the most creative, or even the best at starting new endeavors, but they are not exactly the wisest. In a metaphor related to shooting practice, I heard that entrepreneurs most often take on a new business in this order: *shoot, point, aim.* I am not a gun enthusiast, as I'm a pure yogi and pacifist by nature. But I'm quite sure that if I were faced in a situation where I had to shoot a gun, I don't think *shoot, point, aim,* would be the best strategy for success. However, the metaphor brings about truth in my case. That's exactly how I jumped into my yoga business.

The year was 2007. I was separated in preparation for a divorce. I was formerly a high school language teacher, but had been a stay-at-home mom for several years. I knew I needed a new career to support my three children and myself. But I knew the role of mom was my priority, so I wanted a flexible career that wouldn't take me away from the house for extended periods of time. I had been practicing yoga since 1989 and was passionate about teaching others the practice that had transformed my life at age eighteen. I also wanted to become an Ayurvedic practitioner, since Ayurveda had helped me heal when I was diagnosed with thyroid cancer. My goal was to help people *and* make a living.

With my part of the proceeds from our home sale, I embarked on a journey to take teacher training at the Chopra Center in Carlsbad, California. I figured if I was going to get training, I might as well get it from the best. Twenty thousand dollars later, I received teaching certificates in yoga, meditation, and Ayurveda. My motivation for earning money came from the fact that I had just spent a ton of it on training.

Yet, I had zero business experience. I asked my sister, who runs a one woman industrial design business, how I should incorporate my business, and she suggested an S corporation, which ultimately saved me from further financial devastation down the road. Other than that, I was running my new business by the seat of my pants.

It never occurred to me to join forces with another person as a business partner. Nope. I was the lone ranger. I had all of the great ideas as to how to make my business phenomenal. I was naive and overly optimistic.

Starting Out

I started out with quite a lot of money in the bank. But that money was supposed to be for living expenses, until I got my business off the ground, as well as business expenses. The first mistake I made was not designating a specific amount to spend on the business. In the beginning, since you have no idea how much things are going to cost and also which marketing techniques are going to work, you end up spending more than you anticipate.

In the beginning, I wanted to get the word out everywhere. To that end, I put ads in local papers (which can be quite costly), and printed out brochures in large quantities. I got fancy software programs I didn't know how to use and bought way too much inventory to sell Ayurvedic products. In other words, my spending was completely disorganized.

However, I did do a few things correctly. I applied to teach at a local gym to get practice and to start having income. I negotiated a per-class rate higher than they offered and got it. My advice to you is to always ask. The worst they can say is "no". I also got on a substitute list at another gym. Next, I went to networking meetings to spread the word and to try and find a space to teach. The studio space, I ended up renting, came through a referral from one of those networking meetings. Then, I got off my butt and did some leg work. I went to churches to see if they would take a 10% donation for renting a room to me for a couple classes per week. The church I found had a preschool inside and for me, that meant I had built in clients. The first day of preschool, they allowed me to handout out flyers to the moms advertising my classes during the morning preschool time.

I ran two to three yoga classes weekly at that church for nearly a year. Another thing I did right was to set my prices and not budge. That, however, changed and I made mistakes on that later down the road. The first year I charged $18 per person per class for pre-registration and $25 to drop in. The higher fee was for more personalized service. I rarely had more than ten students in a class. I also didn't offer any free trial classes. My philosophy is the following. I don't work for free. I have bills to pay and kids to feed. I tell prospective clients who want free classes, "You're taking a class. If you like it, great, if you don't, you had an experience. I get paid and we go our separate ways." As you're creating your yoga business, make a decision about giving a free class or not and stick to your decision.

What worked is that I provided exceptional service. I was (and still am) extremely attentive to my clients. I set up all the mats, blocks, straps, and blankets ahead of time. I give everyone a shoulder rub at the end of class. I talk to every client and learn about them personally. During business hours, I answer emails and texts immediately. I call back my clients within the hour. Being outstanding, in every way, is one of the things that will help you stand out from the seas of yoga teachers in the marketplace.

Spreading Myself Too Thin

The first eighteen months, I truly did spread myself thin. I tried to piece together too many part-time jobs, in various places, to make up my full-time job. It began to wear on me. Here is a list of all of the things I was doing to earn a living while trying to create a successful yoga business:

2-3 weekly yoga classes at the church space I rented
2-3 weekly yoga classes at a dance studio I was renting by the hour
2-3 classes weekly at the gym
Substitute teaching at another gym
Selling Mary Kay cosmetics
Holding Ayurvedic classes and doing one-to-one consultations
1 class at a hospital
1-2 classes at corporations

I'm certainly forgetting some things on that list. In addition, going into year two, I added corporate meetings for Weight Watchers, tutoring French, and leading Meet-up groups to try and get more clients. I remember one evening getting into my car and having no idea where I was going. And that, my friend, is what insanity feels like.

My second major mistake was not putting enough eggs into one basket. When your focus is scattered among many different things, you can never be successful at one thing. Granted, I was getting in the teaching hours. I was becoming an expert at teaching yoga and I could easily do it in my sleep. But I wasn't even coming close to making a living and was watching my savings trickle down each month.

When you spread yourself too thin at work, you still have the rest of your life to worry about. By teaching so many classes, I was wearing my body down. I wasn't focused on eating as healthy as I should have. I didn't feel I was spending enough quality time with my kids, because I was always running off to one class or another. And I barely had time for a social life.

Running a Studio?

After having a near mental breakdown, I made the decision to rent a space and hold all of my classes there. The transition didn't happen overnight, but it did happen. Again, here are the mistakes I made:

1. I was still the lone ranger.
2. I didn't have adequate income to afford the space, so in the beginning I was losing money.
3. I didn't have a big enough following to fill classes.
4. Since I was the only one teaching and the human body can only sustain so much, I couldn't hold enough classes to make a profit.

The costs of running a studio are not insignificant. My space wasn't very big, but you still have to pay electricity, Internet, phone, and equipment. Then, I had the pressures of filling the classes I did have on the schedule. Still, I loved going to one place and one place only. I loved my little studio and decorated it the way I wanted. I liked the fact that it was small, intimate and that it felt more like home than a factory cycling students in and out.

Yet, I didn't understand my own nature when it came to business. By nature, I'm not a salesperson. I can sell, but it's not my forte. Truly, I'm the talent. I'm great with people. In my yoga business, I'm excellent at teaching, presenting, and speaking. I get people motivated, happy, and stress-free. Therefore, I wasn't prepared for the rapid hat-changing tricks you must do when you're an entrepreneur. After teaching an uplifting, spiritual yoga session, I would have to switch hats and become the salesperson, cashier, and accountant. I had a difficult time with this transition. When a client would ask for a discount or ask to pay for the series later, it would not only make me feel uncomfortable, but it would rub me the wrong way. Sometimes I felt certain clients were taking advantage of my niceness. And at times I didn't know where to set boundaries. Over the years I learned, but perhaps I learned a little too late.

Eventually, I added interns and teachers. But I made mistakes in those categories too. Overall, customers were happy and so were the teachers. I was the one who sacrificed myself until I had nothing left to give.

I know what you're thinking, "Hey Michelle, thanks for telling me this 'inspirational" story. Now you've got me all depressed." *Hey yoga teacher, this isn't the end of the story. Get up, get a bite to eat, go take a jog around your house, then come back and hear the rest. Jeez!*

Hitting the Erase Button & Going Back to Zero

When it went down, it went down quickly. I saw it coming, but I didn't know what to do. Without a business partner or business savvy friends, I wasn't even able to get proper advice. I had created a vacuum and went down the black hole with my business until I made the decision. I had to close the studio. I was devastated, scared, and uncertain about the future. But I was also a bit relieved. I knew people would be angry. I tried to give customers a six-week advanced warning to use up remaining yoga packages, but I wasn't able to give refunds. I even went the extra mile and gave some students the opportunity to transfer their packages over to my home classes, even though the business was closing. Still, I wasn't spared the anger and frustration of some. Then, my creditors came knocking on the door demanding money. While there were just a few under the business name, my personal finances took a hit that was much worse. I had depleted my savings completely to try and save the business, to my own detriment. It was my baby, I had to try and resuscitate it. I had racked up credit cards and had personal loans. As I mentioned, I literally made every mistake in the book.

Yet, when you're doing something good, God gives you grace. I had made the decision to teach some group classes at home. I'm fortunate enough to have a big single family home. So I converted my formal living room to a yoga and barre studio. I spent more money putting up ballet barres and taking a barre certification, but I got rid of all the overhead costs of the studio. The only problem was, I had just made a lot of people angry and had no money left for marketing. As I sat on my couch sobbing and not knowing how I was going to get income, I heard a still small voice say, "Build it and they will come." In an instant, peace came over me. I knew God was with me and it would be okay.

Okay now you can pause and go get some tissue. I know you feel my pain. And wasn't that a beautiful almost ending?

After seven years, I was literally back to where I started. To my merit, I had built up a fairly good reputation and I did have clients who wanted to follow me to my home studio. In addition, over the years I had become well known in my community for being one of the best prenatal yoga teachers around. Currently, I teach about five group yoga classes weekly out of my home. Business is booming and I have no commute. Best of all, I have almost no overhead. I'm probably making more than I did in my best days at the studio. I teach some private classes and go to people's homes. But in no way is it as stressful as it was the first seven years.

In my experience, I gained the gifts of knowledge, experience, and business know-how. Even though my yoga studio wasn't a total success back then, I had the opportunity to be at home much of the time with my kids. I got to see them grow up. And now with my home studio, my youngest, who's thirteen, helps me set up mats and the room partitions and says goodbye to me on the other side of the house. Having my son nearby *and* teaching my classes is the biggest blessing of all.

CHAPTER ONE

Your Yoga Teacher Training Program

YOU MIGHT HAVE ALREADY completed your yoga teacher training, so this might be a moot point. But if you haven't or if you're considering more training, please read this chapter before spending the money.

Choosing the Right Teacher Training

When I began my yoga teacher training in 2007, programs were stricter. They had a lot of requirements and were lengthier. They tended to be more expensive as well. As I mentioned, I did my yoga teacher training with the Chopra Center in Carlsbad, California. It was a 300-hour program. We had to learn a lot about the human body, human anatomy, and health and nutrition. The program was strict and structured, but I loved it. I found I had a solid foundation for teaching yoga as a career.

With yoga's rise in popularity, teacher-training programs began to crop up everywhere. You'll notice many gyms and yoga brands have their own teacher training. Prices have gone down since the early 2000s, but the time required to acquire a yoga certification has also been compressed. I paid about $7,500 for my yoga teacher training plus travel, hotel and expenses. Today, you can get a 200-hour certification for anywhere between $3,000 and $3,500.

Choosing the right training for you will largely depend on what you want to do with your certification after you graduate.

Reasons for Choosing a Program

Right now you might not have a clear plan for teaching yoga. Take some time and think about what you'd like to do with your certification. As I said, it's a big investment of time and money. You want to make sure you're choosing the right program for you.

You want to work for a specific studio.

I get it. Your local yoga studio introduced you to yoga. You love the environment, community, and vibe and you want to give back. And it wouldn't hurt to have free classes on your days off either. If you're absolutely sure that you don't want to teach anywhere else or specialize in another type of yoga, this might be the route for you.

Basically, if you're trained in a certain style such as Bikram, hot Vinyasa flow, or power yoga, you'll have a difficult time teaching other styles. Here's why. Most of the community-at-large are beginners. I'm going to give you ideas on how to make a living outside of a traditional yoga studio. But in order to be marketable and liked by those who are not tiny and flexible, you're going to have to learn a little bit more on taking care of beginners and people with all kinds of body types.

Another thing to think about is how much you want to get paid per class. Many really popular yoga studios don't pay very well. I was talking the other day with a yoga teacher friend in San Diego, California and he told me that his favorite yoga studio only paid teachers $20 per class. *Yikes! I was paying way too much for my yoga teachers by starting them at $40 per class. I'll bet you want to work for me now, don't you? Well too bad, because I closed my studio, remember?*

You want to open a yoga studio.

If you know you're going to open a yoga studio, be as targeted and specialized as possible. Obviously, if you're opening a franchise, you must teach the style of that franchise. The selection for teacher training will be easy for you. If you're opening a yoga studio, with a brand that allows you the freedom to integrate other types of classes, don't worry about your own training. Hire specialists who already teach those types of classes. For example, if you want barre fitness classes at your studio, hire a barre teacher. Do you want to add prenatal yoga? Add a prenatal yoga specialist. You're going to be too busy running your own studio. You cannot be a jack-of-all trades. You will be a master-of-none and your business will suffer. Focus on your strengths. Let's say you're a pro at hot vinyasa flow. Teach that and then use your other time to focus on your business and client relations.

You want to make teaching yoga your career.

I would recommend you get classic yoga training if you want to make yoga your career. Classic yoga training would include Hatha yoga, some Iyengar yoga or Anusara yoga. The reason you want classic training is to be able to make yourself the most marketable everywhere. Teaching beginners is much, much harder than teaching people who are young, flexible, and experienced. You have to make sure your students don't inure themselves. You have the predicament of teaching in confined spaces, such as office space, classrooms, or senior living homes. You'll have clients who have injuries, have just had surgery, or have special needs. You need to be able to think on the fly when a student tells you about a specific illness or recent injury.

My Chopra Center training combined Hatha yoga, Iyengar yoga, and Raja yoga. I'm so grateful to have had that type of training because I was able to teach in a various number of settings. I have taught students from ages 6 to 93. I have taught people in wheelchairs and those with recent knee surgeries. I've taught moms after C-sections and a client on a respirator. One of the most important parts of my classic training was learning how to properly teach pranayama, yoga breathing techniques. That alone is marketable as a separate class or course. You can help more people with classic training than with any other type of yoga teacher training.

I will add that if you want to volunteer your time teaching yoga in hospitals, at women's shelters, at rehab centers, or at prisons, classic yoga training will also be the best for the same reasons listed above.

You want to take yoga teacher training for personal development.

I've met plenty of teachers who initially take yoga teacher training because they want to improve their practice, learn more about yoga, and enjoy time with other yogis. Personal development is a great reason to take teacher training. If that's your true goal, the sky is the limit. Go all out and take a teacher training in Bali or India. You might as well enjoy the place while taking time for you.

Elements of a Great Teacher Training Program

Teacher training programs registered with Yoga Alliance in the 200-RYT trainings, must meet certain requirements. Yoga Alliance 200-hour standards show that a teacher-training program must contain:

1. Techniques, training, and practice for 100 hours. This includes asanas, pranayama, mantras, meditation, and other yoga techniques.
2. Teaching methodology for 25 hours. This includes communication, demonstration, teaching styles, the student learning process, and the business aspects of teaching yoga.
3. Anatomy and physiology for 20 hours.
4. Yoga philosophy, lifestyle, and ethics for yoga teachers for 30 hours. This includes the yoga sutras, ethics for yoga teachers, and the value of teaching yoga as a service.
5. Practicum for 10 hours.

6. Remaining hours and electives. Yoga Alliances gives each teacher training program the liberty to disperse the rest of the hours among the five categories.

At least 125 hours total must be contact hours. Yoga Alliance describes a contact hour as time spent in the physical presence of a faculty member. In other words, the other hours, or non-contact hours, may be spent on home study, attending yoga classes in other studios, webinars, emails, or conference calls.

In order to be certified, all yoga teachers in training must complete CPR and first aid training.

My suggestion to you: If you've never completed a Red Cross CPR and First Aid class in a classroom setting, do that instead of taking an online course. *Don't mess around people! Someone could drop dead in front of your eyes. You have to know how to save them. Or almost dead, or just unconscious. Or it could be someone who's just messing with you because they were bored in class. Or maybe they just wanted to be in sivasana for the whole class. You never know. Just go practice on a few dummies and you should be good to go. No, I didn't mean your friends. I meant the Red Cross test dummies. Oh goodness, just keep reading.*

Evaluating Training Courses

We've already established that you're spending a big chunk of change on a teacher-training course. You want to make sure the instructors are well qualified and have a lot of experience. With the rate at which teacher training programs have been cropping up in the last few years, you can't be guaranteed to have experienced lead teachers.

So you might be wondering how much is enough experience to train other teachers. That's a good question. We could assign it a number, like five years of teaching. But then you need to think about how much they've taught. If they've been teaching one to two classes per week for five years, with an average of 48 teaching weeks per year, that's only 480 hours of teaching. When I was teaching nearly every waking hour, as a business owner, I taught an average of ten classes per week. Over five years that equals 2,400 teaching hours, which is quite different.

You might have to go by other data, such as whether or not the lead teacher is a studio owner, whether they've been teaching longer on a consistent basis, or if they have credentials through some others means. Look also at how long the studio has been open. Are you planning on taking a teacher training course from a studio that has only been open a year or two? A lot of studios will try to generate more income by having teacher-training programs, but that doesn't necessarily make them good.

Lastly, look at how long the actual teacher-training program has been around. Have they graduated several years of students? Do they have reviews and testimonials from previous students? Are they willing to give out some students' names and numbers so you can call them to get feedback? A good and professional program will not hesitate to give you that information.

Is Advanced Training Necessary?

Many yoga teachers get hooked on taking training programs. They finish the 200-hour yoga teacher training and they want to move on to another. Then, they set their sights on specialty training programs and before you know it, they've spent upwards of $20,000 on yoga training.

I know taking yoga training programs feels good. It's amazing to be among great lead teachers, your peers, and being immersed in the educational setting. Some teachers like to keep the momentum going. They feel that if they get out of the learning mode, they won't go back. While that might be true, look at a couple of things before registering for advanced training.

Do you want to continue your training because you don't feel ready or qualified enough to teach?

If this is the case, start teaching anyway. Or you can intern at a yoga studio for free, with a lead teacher, who's willing to teach you his or her techniques and tricks. I used to train recently certified teachers at my studio. They would intern with me for six-weeks. At the end of that time, if I felt they were ready to teach at the studio, I would hire them. When in doubt, ask. Many of the interns I found called me first, asking if they could be my apprentice.

Do you feel it would increase your income?

If that's your belief, then don't take advanced training. Please don't do it unless you have the money lying around to afford the extra training. It will take time to get a return on investment for the initial $3,500 you spent on your first training. There are many things you can do to build on your 200-hour training. You can read books, watch YouTube videos, buy actual DVDs with those who specialize in areas that interest you, or you can offer to volunteer for a center that has a certain style you want to learn. The certificate will not be worth the money. There is obviously one exception to this rule. If you plan on running a Yoga Alliance 500-hour RYT training, you must have the certification first.

Make Yourself Well-Rounded

A well-rounded teacher is much more marketable. For example, after my teacher training, I traveled to a few of Deepak Chopra's events and taught yoga and meditation. Since 2014, I've been writing articles for Chopra Lifestyle. Being able to put those two things on my resume has added credibility and value to my yoga teaching. Now that I'm a well-known author in the field of Ayurveda, it makes me even more marketable. Do you see how stacking experience can add value to what you do? When you add value, you can charge more for your services and make a better living.

Read books on the yoga sutras, meditation, or read about famous yogis such as B.K.S Iyengar. Take classes with the masters. Attend a few yoga conferences. Learn about Ayurveda. Read about the latest research on yoga, meditation, and mind body health. Continue your yoga education off the mat. So when clients ask you questions, you're well informed. And if you don't know the answer, never, ever, give them advice or guess. Clients look up to you as an authority figure. If you don't know the answer, tell them. You can simply say, "I don't know the answer to that, but I will research it and let you know."

Finally, have other interests in your life so you can successfully talk to clients about other things. A lot of yoga teaching is networking. You really want to get to know people on a personal level. If all you can talk about is yoga, meditation, the chakras, and kriyas, you will be limited in your connection with others. Building relationships is about rapport.

Let me give you an example. I love running and a few years ago, I decided to go for the gold. *No, not the olympics. Get serious!* My sister and I had registered to run the Disney Princess Half Marathon. One day before class, I was talking about my half marathon training. One of my students piped up and said, "I run half marathons and marathons for Run Disney." I told her about my upcoming race at Disney World. As it turns out, she was running the same race. That connection alone made her a faithful client of mine to this day.

Recap of Lessons Learned: Yoga Teacher

Training

1. Before you invest in a yoga teacher-training program, decide what you want to do with your certification.

2. Do your research before enrolling in a teacher-training course. Contact previous students of the program you'd like to join and get feedback.

3. Try teaching for at least a year before getting advanced training.

4. Keep on learning after your certification program. Read books about yoga philosophy, study meditation and Ayurveda. Learn about other health-related topics so you can be well rounded as a teacher.

CHAPTER TWO

You Are Not a Monk, Unless You Are One

Many associate yoga with a rejection of the world, its responsibilities, and commitments, and with extreme austerity leading even to self-mortification. But is not the greater challenge and greater fulfillment to be found living in the world with its tribulations and temptations, and at the same time to maintain both balance and self-control in the everyday life of a householder? - B.K.S. Iyengar, Light on Life, 2005

WHILE THAT MAY SEEM to be a funny chapter title, I feel the need to have this conversation with you. Many yoga teachers feel moved spiritually to share the gift of yoga with others. In that spiritual desire, many also feel they shouldn't take money for teaching or should take less money than they deserve. B.K.S. Iyengar wrote in his book, *Light on Life*, on the challenges of being a yogi and what he calls a "householder". Iyengar, the father of modern yoga, was married, had children, and a demanding yoga business. Yet, being a householder doesn't make you less spiritual, it can actually challenge you to become more spiritual.

Unless you've taken the vow of poverty and are living in a monastery, ashram, or other religious home, where your room and board are paid for, you have bills and expenses like the rest of us. You have needs, wants, and desires. Denying them doesn't make them go away. It will actually magnify them. Have you ever tried to ignore a persistent toddler? It's really hard. The more you ignore, the more they persist. Your needs and desires are the same way. If you're denying your own needs others will "read" this and your teaching will be affected by it. Remember you're carrying your energy with you wherever you go and you're also releasing that energy into the room where you teach.

The inverse is also true. If you go into the yoga business as your cash cow because you read, in the New York Times, that yoga is one of the fastest growing and most lucrative businesses in the West, your insincerity will also seep through.

It's completely fair to have the balance of providing a service to others, being extraordinary, and making a living doing it. You must not feel ashamed or bothered to ask for money for the services you provide. That being said, it's important to understand why you're choosing to become a yoga teacher. The reasons will also help you create your niche audience.

Why Are You Choosing to Teach Yoga?

Now is the time to get completely honest with yourself. *Don't worry it's just you and me here right now. I'm in my pajamas, honestly.* Take time and meditate on the reasons you want to teach this spiritual practice. I'm going to offer a list of ideas to get your thoughts flowing. There are no right answers, only your answers. You will probably have several reasons.

I remember exactly when I knew I wanted to teach yoga. I was pregnant with my third child and yoga had helped me tremendously throughout my pregnancy. I knew then that I wanted to teach prenatal yoga. The interesting part of that story is that I did start teaching prenatal yoga, in 2008. But at the time, I was more focused on teaching regular Hatha yoga. Then, when my business crashed and I brought my yoga classes home, guess which part of my business boomed? Yes, that's right, my prenatal yoga classes! The reason I wanted to teach was, in fact, my path to success. Had I known that several years ago, I would have placed more focus on teaching prenatal yoga.

That's why it's essential for you to get clear on your reasons. Start now!

Exercise: Get out a notebook and pen or grab your computer and open up a word processing document. Take a few deep breaths and relax your body. Think back to the moment during which you decided you wanted to become a yoga teacher. What were your feelings, thoughts, and desires? How did your body feel as you made this decision? What did your mind tell you? What did you see yourself doing after getting your teacher certification? Who did you see yourself helping? When you have a clear picture, open your eyes and write down those reasons.

Below is a list of reasons to get your thoughts flowing.

- I want to give back to my community.
- I want to teach children.
- I want to volunteer my time.
- I want to change careers to teaching yoga.
- I want to expand my yoga practice.
- I want to supplement my income.
- I want to teach at the yoga studio where I learned.
- I want to open a yoga studio.
- I'm a stay at home mom or dad and I want to work a few hours per week.
- I want to keep my full-time job and teach a couple of yoga classes weekly.
- I want to teach yoga to my kids.
- I want to teach prenatal yoga.
- I want to teach yoga at my child's school.
- I want to help others heal.
- I want to teach yoga as a spiritual practice.
- I want to teach yoga as an exercise program.
- I want to teach yoga at work.
- I want to teach yoga abroad or at an all-inclusive resort. (Yes, this is possible.)

- I want to teach senior citizens yoga.
- I want to get fit.
- I want to teach to stay disciplined in my practice.

Now that you've compiled a list of reasons as to why you want to teach yoga. You need to get into the right mindset about your reasons.

Getting Into the Right Mindset

When your heart is set in the right place, there are no wrong reasons to teach yoga or any other spiritual practice. As a leader, your first goal must always be to love and serve others. In fact, a mantra you can repeat to yourself before every class is, How can I help? And how can I serve? You want to keep in mind that you're there to serve. During your yoga teaching time and before and after class, get your ego out of it. Clear your mind and look for ways you can make each client feel special. It doesn't take much. You can give a smile, look into a client's eyes, or offer a blanket or yoga block. Sometimes while adjusting a student, I will whisper into her ear, "How are you doing today?" or some other kind words to show her I care. If you are genuine in your approach and teaching, your students will know it.

Next, accept that all the other reasons you want to teach are equally valid. It's fine that you want to run a business or open a studio. It's also fine if you want to supplement your income or get free classes at your studio for teaching once or twice per week. You will be a much better teacher if you're true to yourself and the reasons you're teaching yoga.

Overcoming Poverty Consciousness

You will have a difficult time making a living teaching yoga, if you don't change your poverty consciousness. You'll become frustrated and harbor resentment and anger and it will affect your teaching. There are many ways you can feed poverty consciousness. Here are some examples.

You just finished teaching a fantastic class. You're feeling great, but also a bit worried because your mortgage payment is due in three days. The month hasn't been as lucrative as you had hoped. One student, who promised to pay for the class session after class, comes up to you and says, "Hey, thanks for a great class. I know I owe you $180 for this session, but I'm running a little short on money this week. Can I pay you next week?" You feel empathy for her and hesitantly say, "Oh, sure. I know you're good for it." In this example you played the martyr. Even though it may not seem apparent, you sacrificed yourself and your needs for hers. You provided a service to her and now your mortgage payment will likely be late and you will pay the consequences because you were too nice. As a result you will suffer from stress, resentment, anger, and frustration.

Another example of poverty consciousness is not charging enough for your services. You feel an internal struggle. You know your students need yoga for better health, but you don't want to burden them with charging too much to take classes. After all, the studio down the street has a special of $49 unlimited. Even though you can only fit 20 students in a class and they can fit 50 students, you feel compelled to offer the same deal.

You are worth the services you provide. Charge what the market can bear and if you're exceptional, charge a bit more. You might attract a lower number of students, but the ones you do attract will be quality. I learned the hard way that students coming to you who are only looking for deep discounts, are not as loyal.

Finally, poverty consciousness comes packaged as this statement I've heard all too often, "I'm teaching a spiritual practice. Shouldn't spirituality be free?"

Think about all of the things you have in life and all the things you do. How many of them are free? Even if you go to a church, synagogue, or mosque, they're not free. Do they not ask for donations at some time during the service and encourage you to give 10% of your salary? Spiritual centers have bills to pay just as you do. Make a list now of all the expenses you have each month. Don't forget anything. Include your yoga clothes, yoga mat, the gas you need to put into your car to get to your yoga classes, the toll you must pay on the highway, the cost of the babysitter while you teach, the carryout food you must bring to your family because you were teaching late, and so on. You need to take care of you. And the only way you will take care of you is if you charge for the services you provide.

When you live in poverty consciousness, whether you're aware of it or not, you become a victim. You're giving away your power to someone else or something else. Teaching spiritual practices takes a lot out of you physically, emotionally, and spiritually. Yes, you do receive back for giving, but it's usually a lot more lopsided, especially if you're teaching upwards of ten classes per week or more. I've noticed my energy level increase when I know I'm being adequately compensated for my teaching. I give a lot more energy to my classes. I'm in a better mood. I give 1000% more because I know I can go home, pay my bills, and rest easy knowing that I'm not struggling to make ends meet.

Back in January 2017, I was struggling to pay some bills. Out of the blue I had a call from a client who wanted private prenatal yoga classes in her home. I charge quite a bit for private lessons and so I wanted to make sure I heard her correctly. She confirmed that she wanted two private classes per week at her home throughout her pregnancy. When I learned where she lived, I hesitated a little because it was a 45-minute drive from my home. But her commitment meant I could pay my bills for the month and then some. Twice a week I found myself happily driving 45-minutes each way to teach her and giving so much more of myself because of how grateful I was for her business. When you're taken care of, it makes the world of difference in how you're able to serve others.

Value Yourself & What You're Offering to Others

By teaching yoga, you're offering something of great value. Think back to all of the things you gained when you first started taking yoga and as you developed in your practice. How has your life been transformed? What has changed for you in your physical, mental, and spiritual health? How have your relationships improved? How has your work life been?

Many teachers I know felt driven to teach yoga because a great teacher had influenced them. Perhaps a yoga teacher helped them overcome anxiety, get out of a toxic relationship, or heal from cancer. You're not just a yoga teacher. You're a spiritual guide and enlightened one.

Do you know what the word *guru* signifies? It means "dispeller of darkness". Students of yoga often refer to their teachers as gurus. Some even assign the term of endearment, *Guruji*, to a special teacher. As you teach yoga, the title "Group Fitness Instructor" doesn't even represent one percent of what you provide. You're a dispeller of darkness. You help your students see the light within them. You help them connect to their spiritual selves. You bring about the true yoga within them, which is the "yoking" or "union" of each student's body, mind, soul, and spirit.

Not to pressure you, but with this role in mind, take your job seriously. You are transforming lives.

My first yoga teacher, Lee Ann Louis-Prescott, is the reason I teach yoga. Lee Ann was my tenth grade high school religion teacher at my catholic high school. In the spring semester of my senior year, I found out she taught yoga at a local community center so I registered. At the time I had no idea what yoga was, but I heard it was good. Lee Ann is a phenomenal teacher who influenced me to fall in love with yoga at the first asana. I was eighteen and had no idea how yoga would change my life. It was all thanks to this little lady, of four feet eleven inches, who had a passion for what she taught. Most of the time you never get to thank the teachers who greatly influence your life. However, a serendipitous event allowed me to thank Lee Ann when I was 38-years-old.

I was getting my third and final certification for my Vedic Master certificate at the Chopra Center. The final program for meditation was a weeklong teacher training. I was studying Sanskrit terms, in the courtyard, at La Costa Resort and Spa. The hour prior I had been in class. We were working on introductions, a little five-minute explanation of how we got into teaching meditation. I was one of the students who had stood up to read my introduction. I had explained how I had taken yoga with my high school religion teacher and that she was the reason I was practicing meditation. Reflecting upon this and tired of studying, I made my way into the Chopra Center gift shop to do a little shopping. *Of course, I'm a woman and that's the way we take a break.* Out of the corner of my eye I saw a small woman, in a bathrobe with a towel wrapped around her head, walking behind the front desk. A flood of emotion came over me. I rushed to the front desk, pointed at the woman in the bathrobe, and asked the receptionist the client's name. She scrolled through client names, but was taking way too long. The woman was getting away. In a burst of inspiration, I cried out, "Lee Ann!" Immediately the lady turned around. I motioned for her to come over to where I was standing. I was dumbfounded. Still shocked, I explained to Lee Ann that she was my high school teacher and my first yoga teacher. With my voice shaking, I told her that just a few minutes before I had spoken about her to my meditation class. As it turns out, Lee Ann was at the Chopra Center getting Ayurvedic treatments for cancer. I was so happy that I was able to thank her for the major influence she had on my life. The good news is Lee Ann is fully recovered and is no longer teaching high school, but owns a successful yoga studio in Brighton, Michigan. If you're in that area of Michigan, check out her studio: *http://yoga-centerbrighton.com/*. She is hands down, the most phenomenal woman I have ever met.

Maximize Your Time & Give More

With all of this talk about earning money, you might be thinking that I'm against volunteerism. I thought you might be thinking that, so I'm going to address that issue here. The one thing in life we cannot buy back is time. Your time is a precious commodity. Most people don't value the time they have and waste it on useless things like TV, gaming, or social media. In the coming sections I'm going to teach you how to make the most of your teaching time financially, so you have free hours to give away to others.

Let me give you an example. Suppose you must make at least $500 per week teaching yoga. Wouldn't it be more economical to make $100 per class for 5 hours of teaching, than earning $25 per class for 20 hours? If you're able to teach five hours weekly and earn what you need, you will have fifteen extra hours in your week. With those extra hours, you can use a few to teach free classes at schools, prisons, or women's shelters.

Furthermore, aren't there other things you'd also like to do with your time? Maybe you'd like to give more time to your spouse and children. Or maybe you have a fun hobby you'd like to pursue. The most successful people are intelligent with their time and allocate it wisely.

In the next chapter, let's figure out how you'd like to allocate your time teaching and how you'd like to organize the rest of your life.

Recap of Lessons Learned: Your Yoga Business is Valuable

We've already established that you're not a monk and that you do have true expenses in life. *And if you are a monk, I apologize profusely and thank you for your prayers.* Keep in mind the lessons you learned on the value of teaching yoga.

1. Make an honest assessment of the reasons why you want to teach yoga.

2. Keep a mindset of service to others at all times.

3. Crush poverty consciousness and value your gift to teach yoga.

4. You are a true guru, a dispeller of darkness, and you basically rock.

5. Work smart not hard. Maximize your time so you can serve more people.

CHAPTER THREE

Hey Dharma? What's Your Karma?

THE WORD *DHARMA*, OF course, is referring to your purpose in life. The meaning of dharma is "righteous duty" or "virtuous path". Because you chose to teach yoga, it's part of your dharma. Your heart moved you toward this career. But your *karma,* equals your actions. Which actions will you *choose* to do? Those choices are totally within your control.

In the last chapter, we got over the limiting beliefs that you need to give without receiving. You conquered poverty consciousness and are ready to make a living teaching yoga. Now let's outline which activities you're going to do.

This is an important step. I made the mistake of saying, "Yes!" to everyone. Yes is a great word. But you can't be like a leaf blowing in the wind. You need direction and vision as to where you want to go.

When people find out you're a yoga teacher, they get excited. You might hear, "Hey, could you volunteer at my kid's school?" Or a neighbor might say, "Do you want to teach at my home? I'll get a few friends to come." When you're starting out and people respond to you this way, you feel wanted. You feel flattered, ecstatic, and enthusiastic. And that's just on the outside. On the inside you're saying to yourself, *On top of it, I'm pretty hot. Of course they want me, so I have to say yes.* And because you haven't planned your teaching time and your ego is a bit puffed up, you answer, "Sure! I'd love to!" Then before you know it, you're overcommitted and underpaid.

Yoga Teaching Time

How much time you spend teaching yoga is going to depend largely on many factors. First of all, how much time do you want to spend teaching? Be realistic. My lead teacher at the Chopra Center, Claire Diab, told us she made a living teaching yoga when no one thought it was possible, back in the 1980s and 90s. She taught 25 classes per week. To me, that's insane! I shared with you earlier that, on average, I taught about ten classes weekly. My threshold for teaching yoga is about twelve classes per week. After that my body shuts down and I tend to get sick or over exhausted.

When you think about teaching time, you must add prep time, set up, and clean up time. In the beginning, you will spend an hour or two prepping for one class.

It seems like a lot, but it's worth it. After the first year I had about eight solid class outlines memorized. Solid class plans made it much easier moving forward. After you have prepared your class, you need to get there. Don't forget to add travel time. You will want to arrive about twenty minutes early and stay twenty minutes afterward. So if you're teaching a one-hour class, it's really an hour and forty minutes plus commute. In my example, my twelve-class week looks a little more like 24 hours instead of twelve. But some of my classes are 75-minutes and others are 90-minutes. So realistically, my twelve classes come closer to 26 hours. Do you see where I'm going with this? A regular workweek is 40 hours without the commute. Without my commute, my twelve classes are nearing a full-time job. I hope that gives you some perspective. Now you know why I want you to be able to maximize your time.

Let's suppose you want to teach ten classes per week. And you'd like to cap your classes at one hour each. We've already agreed that you need to double that to 20 hours. Next, you need to find the gaps in your day when you can teach. In my experience, most people want yoga in the evenings and on weekends. I've tried day classes. Sometimes they work well and other times I get no one. The problem with the popular times is that if you ever want to see your boyfriend, girlfriend, spouse, or kids *and* make a living teaching yoga, something is going to have to give. But before I get ahead of myself, let's work with the example of teaching ten classes.

You make a decision that you will teach Monday, Tuesday, and Thursday evenings. On one of those days you will try to teach two classes back-to-back. Now you have four classes on your schedule. Then, you decide you want to teach a lunchtime class at noon on Tuesdays and Thursdays, which equals six. Since weekends are popular, you will schedule two classes on Saturday mornings, and now you have eight scheduled. You're going to leave the last two slots open for private clients and will actively seek out clients to fill those spots. And there you have it!

Now that you've solidified your teaching time, don't deviate from it. Here's why. If you have a family, which I assume you do, it's only fair to them that they know when they can see you. And if you have kids, you might need to make arrangements for childcare. The one running issue I had was with my son's soccer schedule. Because of my teaching hours, classes always conflicted with a soccer practice or game. Knowing my yoga schedule allowed me to ask for help from others ahead of time.

Your Teaching Action Step List

Your schedule is solidified or you have a rough draft of what your schedule will look like. Now, you must decide what kind of yoga teacher you want to be.

Before teaching yoga, I taught middle and high school French and Spanish. When I started out, I wanted to be the perfect teacher. I thought back to all of my past teachers and the cool things they did to motivate us in class. Before you knew it, I had about a hundred cool things I was going to do as a teacher too. I set out to be Super Teacher. I had visions of teacher-of-the-year awards and all of my students worshipping the ground I walked on. And of course, they were all going to speak French and Spanish perfectly. As a result, I went crazy with my shopping list. I filled my cart with all of the neat teaching supplies and gadgets to decorate my classroom. I had the best language games to play with my students, and prizes to reward them. Oh boy, did reality hit me super fast. By doing all of the "cool" things I wanted to do, I didn't get much solid teaching time done. My transitions were sloppy because students were over stimulated from my awesome games. Furthermore, I crammed way too many things into one lesson. And what else did I learn? My students didn't worship me. *To my dismay.* Many of them loathed me. *And how dare they?* They didn't love French and Spanish as much as I did. *C'est dommage!* Taking French or Spanish was part of a language requirement. After the first few months of teaching, my heart was crushed.

Your yoga students probably want to be there, unless they're children put in your class by pushy parents. In other words, the great thing about working with adults is that they come to yoga because they want to. But they might not love yoga as much as you do. Some students might be there because their doctor or physical therapist told them to go. But as far as teaching goes, please learn from my past teaching mistakes. You don't have to be Super Yogi Guruji to be a good teacher. *I should make that a T-shirt: Super Yogi Guruji, 'Taking You to Higher States'.*

I had a great yoga teacher in Virginia, who was a quirky, eccentric guy. He was a motorcycle loving Vietnam vet with long hair, tattoos, a nice smile, and gentle voice. He went all in with his teaching. He would play the flute at the end of class, have these crazy routines and was embarrassingly frank. He would tell us, "If you gotta pass gas, just let it out all out man, it's natural." He was a hoot. As fantastic as he was, I could never, ever be like him in a million years. He was crazy popular, but I had to find my own style.

When I started teaching yoga I created a class format that I stuck to. I had formed set sections and plugged in the poses I wanted to teach in those sections. I always start with breathing techniques and a yoga principle for the day. During *sivasana*, I give every single student a shoulder adjust, shoulder rub, and blessing. In the beginning I would use hand towels to cover all of the students' eyes. After a few months, I realized that took too long. I have a cue for the students, who want to be covered up with a blanket during sivasana, so I'm not needlessly covering every student. At the end of class I always say exactly the same thing and I've been saying it for nine years. I don't try to find fancy poems, inspirational sayings, or light a million candles. I learned that in teaching, less is more.

In order to find your action step list, figure out what you absolutely want to do as you teach class. Below are some actions to think about:

- Do you want to play music?
- Do you prefer silence?
- Do you want the room lit by candlelight?
- Do you want to read poetry at the end of class?
- Do you want to teach large or small classes?
- Do you like teaching in extreme heat?

- Are there inspirational quotes you'd like to read to your students at the end of class?
- What styles are you open to teaching?
- Do you want to set up your classroom perfectly before the students come in?
- Do you want to give adjustments to every student during sivasana?
- Do you want to use yoga blankets, blocks, straps, and bolsters or do you want to keep it simple?
- How many poses do you strive to teach in one class?
- Do you want to teach your students more about stretching and relaxation or strength?
- Do you believe the purpose of yoga is more about getting fit than relaxing? If so, will you include hand weights?

Imagine what you want to do and compile a list. Don't make this too stressful. Have fun with it.

What Is Your X Factor?

Let me tell you a secret. You don't teach who you want to be, you teach who you are. Even if you want to emulate a LuLu Lemon cover model and inside you're a modern hippie (like me), that is what's going to come out. As much as I tried to fit into the modern gym yoga teacher scene, that's not who I am and so I didn't do a very good job of it. I'm more spiritual, empathetic, intuitive, and connecting. It was stressful to have a group fitness studio filled with forty students because I couldn't connect to all of them. And when they figured out I wasn't like most teachers, my classes got smaller, which wasn't good for me or for the gym. I had to embrace who I am and work with it. I had to find my X factor.

The great news is, because I'm so different, I'm unique in the sea of modern yoga teachers. And so it was pretty easy to find my X factor. In business this is also referred to as your USP, Unique Selling Perspective. If you're more like the modern gym yoga teacher, you will have a more difficult time finding yours. But please try. Ask a couple of good friends, who know you well, about your unique personal strengths. Running any successful business (and yes, even if you are one person, you're still a business) requires finding the one or two things that sets you apart from your competition. You must do this or you will not rise above the crowd.

One way, to figure out your X factor is to start with your audience. What group are you attracted to teaching? For me, the first group was women between the ages of 40 and 55. Then, my next group was pregnant women. I built on my demographics to see how I could best serve them.

Once you have your demographic or sub-group, notice how you interact with them. What makes you special and gives you a connection to them that no one else does as easily? You might work well in small groups of students versus large groups. Or maybe you have a unique way of explaining yoga poses. For me, I'm kind of dorky and funny. In the middle of class when it gets too quiet or serious, I'll say something funny. For example, in my prenatal yoga class I'll say, "Have you ever noticed that your feet grow during pregnancy?" That breaks the seriousness. The women laugh and then one will tell the story of how she just tried to buy a pair of shoes and had to buy a size bigger.

Focus on your strengths and magnify them. The more you practice what you're good at, the more pronounced your X factor will become.

What Are Your Priorities in Life?

Each one of us has top priorities in life. It doesn't make one priority right and the other wrong, it's just reality. I already mentioned that my top priority was my kids. That made it difficult to have a successful yoga studio when I was the only one teaching. I taught classes, but I wanted so much to be at home with the kids that I didn't add enough classes or rushed home after class. Currently, even though I only have one remaining child at home, teaching classes there and having my writing career is a much better fit.

If your top priority is money and financial security, don't quit your day job to teach yoga. And don't be embarrassed to admit that money is a top priority. If it's real for you, own it. When I first opened my studio, the owner of a very successful studio invited me over to talk. She gave me some tips and asked me how I was doing. I confessed that it was difficult to make a profit. She laughed and said, "Luckily our husbands make a lot of money; otherwise we wouldn't be able to survive." Even after ten years in business, she still wasn't able to make a living wage for our area.

Marriages also take a toll when you teach yoga full time or run a yoga studio. Remember, you'll be teaching at the popular times, nights and weekends. If your spouse works during the day and you work in the evenings, you're going to be tag teaming and not seeing each other as often. In late 2008, when I started my yoga business, but didn't have a studio space, I met another teacher who had opened her yoga studio in the beginning of the year. Her space was beautiful and in a high demand shopping center. I can't even imagine what her monthly rent must have been. She had a great concept for a yoga studio, family yoga. She held classes for couples, kids, and families as well as the traditional offerings. Married with three kids, she quickly realized that the demands of the studio kept her away from her family. At the one-year anniversary, she didn't say, "The studio made it through the first year." She said, "Our marriage made it through the first year." Her studio also had financial backers. But eighteen months after she opened, I heard she was closing. We talked about six months after she closed and she said, "I'm so much better now. I get to see my kids at night. I get to see my husband. I didn't realize how stressful it was for my marriage and my whole family."

I'm not saying this to scare you. I'm sharing this to give you a dose of reality. I would be insensitive to not warn you of the stress and absenteeism you will feel if kids, family, and marriage are your top priorities. The best-case scenario would be to open a yoga studio with your spouse. It's a financial risk, but if you work well together, you'll have the best of both worlds.

If you're career oriented, you've got it made. You'll be very successful in your yoga business. You'll be motivated to make it work and be proud of the rewards.

Now that you know more about yourself and how you're going to teach, let's explore how to build your reputation as a yoga teacher.

Recap of Lessons Learned: Action Steps

1. Decide which days and times you will teach and how many hours you'll dedicate to class hours weekly.

2. Write down the top three things you absolutely want to do when you teach. Think about environment, style, and little extras to make your students feel special.

3. Pinpoint one or two assets that make you stand apart from the crowd.

4. Admit to yourself and at least one other person your top priority in life. Understand that your top priority will lead the trajectory of your yoga business.

CHAPTER FOUR

Building a Reputation

Unless you've been teaching other classes, building up your reputation as a yoga teacher and business owner takes time. You'll need to impress a few students, build up your following, and start getting great reviews. As you're building your reputation, there are a few things to think about and put into practice.

Create Your Personality

Sounds weird right?

You are who you are. Guess again. This business is strange. When people start on a spiritual path, many seem to believe they must become their gurus or a person they aren't. All of the sudden you're not Suzie from

Brooklyn, you're Star Flower, an enlightened being. And all you want to teach about is love and harmony. You feel everyone should get along, take yoga every day, and give everything to the poor. You start to speak in a breathy, high-pitched and slow voice and begin to annoy everyone around you. *Come on! Get real!*

Emulating a great teacher is wonderful. Now add your flavor to it. I'm super down to earth and real. I like to make fun of myself to make others laugh. I have a theatre background, so from time to time I like to ham it up a bit. *In case you haven't noticed.*

However you decide to present yourself to your students; be genuine. This profession lends itself to sensitivity and students can sniff out an inauthentic teacher, even if they're not in down dog pose.

Keep It Professional

As you're building your reputation and keeping it impeccable, you must keep your relationship with your students completely professional. This rule applies to the yoga teachers you train and those who work under you. I can't emphasize this enough.

You must hold a respective barrier between you and your students at all times. It doesn't matter if they've been your students for one year or twenty. If you don't do this, you will have a difficult time charging them for your services. I've been invited to my students' homes for Christmas parties, an occasional lunch, and tea and coffee. You can accept and go, if you keep that respectful distance. Think about it. When you were a kid, if your

parents invited a teacher or the pastor to dinner, respectful boundaries were always kept. *That is, unless you are
Meggie from The Thorn Birds. Didn't you love that series?*

I hope I'm bringing up the obvious here. Do not, under any circumstances, get romantically involved with
a student or teacher who works for you. It's completely
unprofessional. If romantic interest develops and your
heart tells you to pursue it, have a talk with the person.
Agree that he or she will leave the studio completely first
and then start dating. Otherwise you're setting yourself
up for a possible sexual harassment case or some other
lawsuit if things go wrong. Even if you don't have legal
action taken against you, your studio and your integrity
will be compromised. Remember, you're a business owner first.

Another reason to stay professional is that your students, even if they're older than you, look up to you as
an authority figure. You're not a peer, even if you're the
same age. Furthermore, if the relationship moves past a
respectful distance and turns sour, you've just made a
reputation enemy. What are reputation enemies? They
are disgruntled customers who now have it out to make
you pay. I'm not joking. When it comes to your work and
reputation, be careful. The Internet makes it too easy for
your reputation to be completely ruined in a second. And
bad reviews never go away.

Let me tell you a story of a yoga teacher I trained. She
was much younger than me and completely adorable. We
had formed quite a close bond and she was the first yoga
teacher I hired. We met once month for lunch and then
when other teachers joined, we'd all go to lunch. I made

the mistake of revealing too much about my personal life to her. As time went on she took advantage of our closeness. One time when she was scheduled to teach, a couple of days before a holiday, she asked me to cancel because only two students were on the roster. Then, she became whiny because numbers were down, at some point, and told me that teaching wasn't fun anymore. I was struggling to boost business and dealing with what seemed to be a defiant child instead of my employee. When I called her on it she got upset. Finally she quit. We didn't part on good terms. She said she felt disappointed because I was her mentor and she looked up to me. But when I had to play hardball because I was the boss, after all, she couldn't handle me in that role because of our closeness. I was disappointed with her. But I had to look at myself and see where I had let my professional barriers down. It was a lesson I never forgot.

The No-Nos of Rapport

In this touchy-feely business, it can be difficult to set and keep boundaries. After all, you're making people feel good. You're opening up energy centers and helping people see their spiritual selves. You guide the energy in the room and at times you feel at one with the universe and so do your students. Here's the upside. Creating rapport is easy in this setting. The downside is; if you don't set the thermostat and keep it constant, you can let in too much heat or cold.

Let me explain with this example. You meet with the same group of students every Tuesday night. All of the students get to know each other and they get to know you quite well. One Tuesday, in particular, you have a rough day. Your car broke down, you and your boyfriend got into an enormous fight that might cause a breakup, and your Uber driver showed up late. You arrive to class frazzled. Your students notice this and lovingly ask you what's wrong. Thankful for the their compassion and friendship, you begin to pour out the details of your day. Then ten minutes later you're teaching those same people, who just became your therapists or girlfriends at the bar after a long day's work. It's not fair to them and it's not fair to your image. In other words, leave your emotional baggage at the door before you walk in, each and every time. I tell you this from firsthand experience. Never, in a million years, burden your clients with anything that's going on in your life.

Imagine going to a therapist for a serious matter that must be resolved. You're paying your therapist for 45-minutes of her professional time. Then, instead of letting you talk and giving you guidance, she starts talking to you about her life. Wouldn't you be upset and frankly a little put off? And you might even be thinking, *I just got off at crazy town!*

You might be thinking, "Yeah Michelle, but you know my students love me. They understand. They're human too." Yes, they're human and yes, they most certainly understand. But they're *paying* you to provide a service.

A couple of years ago, I made it a practice to do a little hand swoop around my body to clear out negative energy or thoughts of things that happened during the day. Then I say to myself before class, "Let me bless these students, allow me to help them and get my ego out of it." I take a few deep breaths and go.

Here's another bit of advice. Don't take your cell phone to your yoga mat. If it needs to be there, put it on airplane mode. Even though you might be waiting for a text or call, your students deserve your full attention for the entire class time.

A true story about rapport

My family and I love Disney. We go to Walt Disney World every other year. One thing we love about Disney is the impeccable customer service. You always know, that no matter what, you will have a fantastic time. The place is spotless and the employees are all cheerful and happy. All Disney employees, from the floor sweepers and bathroom cleaners to the ticket handlers are trained to smile, greet you, and ask you how your day is going. It is completely un-Disney-like to see an employee not do this. After several decades of these high expectations, we met one Disney employee who did not embody the rigorous Disney standards. This past summer, my boys and I went to Disney's Vero Beach Resort. We had a difficult time with the remote and couldn't get the DVD player to work. A Disney maintenance guy showed up to our hotel room door and troubleshooted the problem. He was perfectly nice to us, but he started to complain about his superintendent and how she was disorganized and so on. We all stood there flabbergasted. We had never, in all of those years, heard a Disney employee complain about anything. All we had seen were cheery employees with sunny dispositions. It was completely shocking. As he left, my boys and I turned to each other wide-eyed. We couldn't believe what we had just heard.

No complaints

That leads me to my next no-no of rapport. Do not complain about anything. Don't complain about people, places, circumstances, the traffic, or weather, not a single thing. If you have a habit of complaining, stop now. Recently, I was reading this phenomenal book, I would highly recommend, called *The Power of Focus* by Jack Canfield, Mark Victor Hansen, and Les Hewitt. In the book, there's a chapter on formulating good habits and letting go of bad ones. I realized that I had the bad habit of complaining about little things. I never complained so much about the big stuff, just little annoyances. I would complain about the weather or about long traffic lights. While reading this book, I made the decision to lose the complaining habit altogether. It doesn't serve anyone to complain. In the end, it makes you look bad, in the same way we looked at that Disney employee. We didn't think a thing of the woman he was complaining about, we were focused on him and his negativity.

Try not complaining for a week and see how it goes. I've replaced complaining with this phrase, "Hmmmm, this is interesting. Let's see what else I can do about this." Another replacement for complaining is saying five things you're grateful for in the moment. So if I'm stuck at a really long traffic light, *(OMG, in Northern Virginia, they do get really long. And no, that's not a complaint. It's truth!)* and notice that I'm getting annoyed, I'll say, "I'm thankful for..." and list five things. It works!

Gathering a Following

Pretty soon after you start teaching you'll start to gather a core following. The same students will show up to your classes each week. They're the ones who show up early to talk and the ones you need to cherish. You only need a handful of students who become your raving fans.

Your core clients or raving fans are the ones you will rely on for most of your business. The classic business model, for your customer base, shows that 20% of your clients will represent 80% of your business. In my case, that certainly seems to be true. A small number of clients will make a huge difference in how your business grows. These are the clients who will pay for anything and everything you do. They will leave great reviews. They will refer friends and family to you. They're your bread and butter. Cherish them.

You only need about ten to twenty core clients to run a successful yoga business. When you notice who they are, give them a little extra. Give them extra attention. Recommend a book you know they might like. Bring them a cookie or chocolate from home. *Bribe them like crazy! I'm kidding.* In the same way that you're going to develop your natural talents, you're going to focus more energy on your core clients. Don't spend time chasing clients who only show a small interest in your teaching and services. When you place your focus on your raving fans, you'll notice your client base will grow.

Customer Service Nightmares

Luckily, true customer service nightmares are few and far between when you're practicing the principles outlined in this chapter. However, when they do occur, look out and have a strategy. In the nine years I've been teaching yoga, I can count about five major customer service nightmares that were just horrible. They're the kind that keep you up at night.

There are two types of customer service nightmares you'll encounter. The first are policy and money related and the second are customer service related.

In order to never have to deal with policy and money related nightmares with clients, you must have your rules set in stone before you go into business. In other words, decide now what your policies will be regarding payment for classes, your refund policy, class cancellation policy, and make up policy.

I decided early on to have a no refund policy. If you buy a package or service with me, there are no refunds whatsoever, unless it's a charging error. You can exchange classes for another service, but I will not hand money back to you under any circumstances. And once a session starts, you cannot exchange it. Here's why. If you're a sole proprietor, meaning you run your business by yourself, you can't have people deciding on a whim that they don't want your classes anymore. In my experience, people come up with the lamest excuses. Think of "the dog ate my homework" excuses and worse. I've literally heard it all. Many adults are like big kids. They get lazy and want to quit. Or life gets in the way and they just don't want to take classes anymore. Some try to get money back, so they come up with crazy stories. I have had a couple of chargeback requests from clients' credit card companies and have won. The only one I did not win was because I had a new booking system and the client didn't actually sign anything with the "no refund" policy. So my advice to you is, have all clients sign off on your no refund policy if you decide to have one.

The same goes for your class cancellation policy and make up policy. Decide now. Another thing you must decide is if two people or more can share the same yoga pass. Let's say you offer a 10-class package. I've had customers ask if they can share it with a spouse or teenage child. It doesn't bother me, but it might get confusing if too many people use the same pass. Also, make a decision on expiration dates if you sell passes and packages. Stand firm on your decision for 99% of the cases. However, there is always that one percent exception. For example, a client gets hit with the flu for three weeks and you know he's telling the truth. You can offer to extend the pass under exceptional circumstances.

Now with rock solid policies on rules and money, you have the second major reason you might encounter a customer service nightmare and that has to do with service complaints.

You can be a perfect angel and the best yoga teacher around and a client may still find a reason not to like you or your class. It's hard to control all conditions and some people just like to complain or find fault. In that case, try to do everything you can to accommodate without compromising your rules and policies. It gets even trickier when the customer complaint involves one of your teachers.

My Yoga Studio's Customer Service Nightmare

The biggest customer service nightmare I ever encountered, in my entire life, involved all-of-the above, but in different stages. I had a customer who was a raving fan. He was really happy with all of the teachers, the classes, and the studio. He would tell me daily how much he enjoyed the classes and environment. At that time, the studio was starting to pick up and got busy. Classes were full and some students began showing up late. This client began to get annoyed and voiced his opinion. At the end of class he shouted at one of my teachers. The second time students showed up late, he stormed out of the class in the middle of the lesson. After class, he showed up at the door and again shouted at a different teacher. I wasn't in the studio both times, so I had to get the story from two teachers, as well as the client, to figure out what happened. I tried, in earnest, to appease him. I told him I would talk to the teachers and we would rework a policy on late students. He would hear nothing of it. He told me that he wanted me to lock the door of the studio at the beginning of class and not let anyone in. I explained, that for safety issues we could not lock the door. In the end, he left the studio. Later, he tried to get his money back for his membership. It was a long drawn out mess that took a long time to end. If that wasn't enough, he wrote an untruthful and reputation shattering review that remains, on the Internet, to this day.

I learned a few lessons from that experience that I can pass on to you. It's okay to ask a client to leave. I was so blindsided, by his change of heart from a raving fan to a reputation enemy, that I was more interested in keeping him as a client rather than protecting myself, my teachers, and the studio. You can even create a policy, about asking a member to leave the studio with no refunds, for unacceptable behavior. In the end, yelling at my teachers and making irrational policy demands *were* unacceptable. The next lesson I learned was, don't say too much. I got too wordy, giving him too many explanations, and trying to be friendly, rather than being a leader and decision-maker. If you encounter a customer service nightmare, hear everyone's story, make an assessment, make a decision, deliver your verdict, and case closed. There is no negotiating or waffling. It's your business, your livelihood, and your rules.

Be Extraordinary

We have become a society of mediocrity. We give trophies and rewards to all children and for any reason. Degrees and certificates are easier to come by. If you strive to be extraordinary, you will come out ahead from the start. How can you be extraordinary? Live by your values.

Make a list of the values that are near and dear to your heart. Your top values might be honesty, integrity, trustworthiness, punctuality, or generosity. Strive, in every way, to live by those values in and outside of your yoga classes. Practice what you preach.

Study the eight limbs of yoga by Patanjali. Take one of the branches or limbs and study it in earnest one week at a time and then live it. Always aim to do better and to be better. Remain a beginner and never claim you're the expert. The universe is too big, vast, and wide for you to know everything. Finally, stay humble. Humility is the sign of a true leader.

Building Yourself Back Up When You're Down

Real entrepreneurs know the value of failure. Once again, this was a lesson I took a long time to learn. Failure is not the end; failure is feedback. The main reason people don't succeed is because they look at failure as a sign to quit. The most successful people have failed more than they have succeeded. Thomas Edison failed 1,000 times before he successfully made the light bulb. Henry Ford failed and went broke several times before inventing the Model T. Steve Jobs got kicked out of his own company, by a CEO he hired, and had to stay on the outside for twelve years struggling to make himself relevant once again.

Failure is your friend. You must fail in order to succeed. If you're not failing at some point, you're not stretching the limits. You're playing it safe. In business, you will try ideas that won't work. Find out why they didn't work. Where were the flaws in your plans? Were you trying to make a quick buck? Did you offer something you thought your clients needed, but it wasn't something they wanted? There is always a lesson to learn.

I used to get crushed if a student didn't renew a yoga package or stopped showing up to class. I was overly sensitive, wondering what I did wrong or how I could improve my teaching. Self-analysis is always good, but don't overdo it. Sometimes life gets in the way. People have other priorities and demands. At times it's an issue with not having enough money to continue with classes. Other times, they just want to try another activity. Try not to take it as rejection. A good way to find out why they aren't coming back is to ask. Some clients will give you an honest answer and others won't. Either way, you can't let it affect you. Try to take a more philosophical approach. Do you know the expression, *When the student is ready, the teacher will appear?* I've tried to include the opposite of that expression into my personal philosophy. *When the student has learned, it's time for him or her to move on.* If a student moves on, know you've done your job. It's time for another teacher to appear for your client. Send them a blessing and let them go.

At times you're feeling funky because you received a bad review or negative feedback. I know it's a hard pill to swallow. I took pride, in the beginning of my yoga teaching career, that I only had five star reviews. Then I got my first negative review and my world came tumbling down. I took it so personally, that I couldn't shake it off. If and when that happens to you, you need to keep in mind that not everyone is going to like you and that's perfectly fine. You're human. Everyone has different needs and desires. Your teaching style might not be what that client wanted.

I have also found that some people are just really demanding and no matter what you do, they're never happy. Do you know a few people in your life like that? With those people, you have to let them go. Get them out of your energy field. If they come back to your class, you could even suggest another teacher for them who might be a better fit.

Focus on the positive. When you get a good review, celebrate. Absorb the positive feelings your happy students provide. Learn from negative feedback and see if there's a grain of truth. Think about what you can do to improve if it's something within your control. Once you've done that, surround yourself with loving people, those who accept you unconditionally and let them fill you up.

Recap of Lessons Learned: Reputation

1. Be your authentic self onstage and off.

2. Keep a professional demeanor at all times. *No sleeping with the students or underlings.*

3. Set healthy boundaries and keep them.

4. Keep complaints to yourself at all times. Practice gratitude instead. *Thank you very much!*

5. Find your peeps and love 'em to death. *Not to death, really. I didn't mean that. I meant love 'em with cookies and such, but not fattening cookies; vegan, gluten-free, sugar-free, tasteless cardboard cookies, and a little chocolate.*

6. Set your policies and keep them in place. Be a leader. Make decisions about customer service nightmares and don't waffle. *Unless serving waffles is the way you're going to appease the angry customers.*

7. Stick to your values and strive to be extraordinary.

8. Failure is your friend. Pick yourself up off the floor and try something else until you succeed. *Would you treat your students the way you treat yourself? If they couldn't do a pose would you say, "You failed! Stop trying and go home!" Think about it. Treat yourself the way you would treat someone you teach or mentor.*

CHAPTER FIVE

Marketing Your Way to Success

ONE SUBJECT I KNEW absolutely nothing about before starting my yoga business was marketing. Yet, when you start a business, you spend about 50% of your work hours marketing. If you have no idea what you're doing, it can be crazy stressful. When you signed up to be a yoga teacher, all you wanted to do was teach and now most of your time is spent on creative ideas to woo in clients.

In this chapter, I'm going to save you thousands of dollars in mistakes that I made. As far as marketing is concerned, I have tried absolutely everything and I'm not even kidding. I lost so much money by trial and error and as I explained, financially devastated my family and myself. I want to spare you the same pain.

I falsely believed, that in order to run a great business, you had to spend a lot of money on advertising. You do have to spend money, especially in the beginning, but you don't have to spend a lot.

If you plan on teaching most of your classes in a gym or yoga studio, you might be led to believe that you don't need to market. This belief is only partially true. You're still going to have to create relationships with your students and that is marketing. In fact, the essence of marketing is relationship building. Remember, if you work in a gym or studio, your boss or your boss's boss needs to market all of the time. So if you want to be valued, you'll need to provide creative ideas to keep your clients happy and attract new ones. I worked for a high-end gym my first year of teaching and my fitness director was constantly asking me to create classes or workshops to keep my clients' interest.

In order to properly market, you'll need to know your target audience, what they want, and how to reach them.

Your Target Market

Any person entering into business for the first time has grand visions. They are usually so enamored with their product or service, they are under the impression that anyone will want it. Yet, there is always a target audience for a specific product or service with a certain age range, shopping behaviors, lifestyle, marital status, etc. Think about some products you know. Who is Apple's target market? How about Whole Foods Market? Who is the target audience for Walmart? Are they the same audiences across all three brands? As you read the names, a mental image may have come to mind of the type of person who buys those brands. Those are the target markets.

When considering your target audience, think about the following:

- Age
- Gender
- Family size
- Marital status
- Income
- Profession
- Education
- Spending habits
- Hobbies
- Leisure activities

You want to get a clear idea of your target audience before you start marketing. If you're uncertain because you haven't started teaching yet, think about the style of yoga you teach. In your yoga studio or gym, what do the people, who take that style of yoga, look like? What do they wear? What cars do they drive?

What Does Your Target Market Want?

The other day I was on a coaching call with a publicist. I was having an issue attracting my target market for an upcoming seminar. I asked him for advice and he told me, "One thing many entrepreneurs don't realize is that clients want what *they* want and not necessarily what they need." As a business owner, it doesn't matter what I think my clients need. I have to learn what they actually want if I'm going to succeed.

Late last year, the Apple iPhone 7 came out with no headphone jack and a wireless headset. I remember many people were angry, myself included, because we like the ability to use a wired headset if we want. With no headset jack, you can't use one. As a customer, I felt they were messing with something that didn't need to be messed with. When you have a great product and people like it, why mess it up? That's an example of a company deciding what people need, but not giving them what they want.

So how do you know what your audience wants? Ask them! You can conduct a survey. You can create a focus group. Gather ten people, who meet the criteria for your target audience, and ask them what classes they would enjoy, at what times of day, and for what duration. You might get conflicting answers, but you also might get some insight.

Another way to know is to notice. Which classes fill up faster than others? Which months get busy and which ones are slow? Do they prefer long sessions, like a semester long, or short ones?

One time, I had a great client who would sign up for every session. In the fall, of this particular year, I was experimenting with longer sessions. When the client saw the price she exclaimed, "Michelle, I like your classes, but this is getting too expensive for me!" Once I explained to her that the price was for 12 weeks instead of 8 weeks, she registered. Her feedback was helpful to me because

I realized that shorter sessions, with a lower price tag, seem to be more attractive to clients.

How to Reach Your Target Market

Wouldn't it be great if you could just post a few flyers around town and have students flock to your classes? Unfortunately, the reality is that people are so distracted today, that you'll have to find a variety of ways to get their attention. If you've done any job that requires marketing, you know you must have eight touch points with a potential client before they buy. The latest marketing research shows that the touch point number has doubled to sixteen in recent years. The reason is we are so inundated with information that it's difficult to get people to notice.

If you're not familiar with marketing, touch points are marketing efforts to connect with a potential client in any way. A touch point can be a phone call, postcard, email, meeting, YouTube video, social media post, direct mailing, or any other way you can connect.

For the rest of the chapter, I'm going to divide marketing activities into three categories: must-have marketing, free marketing, and paid marketing. My suggestion to you is to plan your marketing in that exact order. Don't jump to paid marketing thinking it will get you quick results, because it won't. I promise.

Must-Have Marketing

Before you start your yoga business, these are the must-haves. They're not free, but I'm going to teach you how to do them at a lower cost. Take these steps while you're still in yoga teacher training if you can. That way, as soon as you graduate, you'll be ready to go.

Company name and branding

In the Business Model chapter, I'll talk about your legal business status. But for now, decide what you will call your yoga business. If you know for certain that you're opening a yoga studio and have a business partner, discuss it together and come up with a name. When I created my business, I came up with a really obscure name, The Ayurvedic Path. I did it because I wanted to be known for Ayurveda on the East coast. It eventually worked to my advantage. However, it seriously affected business for the first several years. Absolutely no one knew what Ayurveda was. So why would they frequent such a business? In retrospect, I made a huge mistake.

Keep your business name simple, direct, and to the point. Potential customers must know what services you're providing at first glance. If you choose a name like *Awesome Asanas,* or something cutesy, it may look good to you, but not to clients searching for yoga. Another thing to keep in mind is that this brand will follow you for a long time. You have to love your yoga business name, because it will be attached to your name forever.

Branding is your logo and other visuals surrounding your business name. If you're not a graphic designer, hire someone to do your logo and branding materials. Have a header and letterhead designed for your website, all so-cial media accounts, and physical printing. Professional branding will cost you upwards of $500 or more. *But you don't have to pay that amount, because you're smart, sexy, and resourceful.* Find a college student, who is majoring in graphic design, and offer $100 and an opportunity to put the work in his or her portfolio. They will work re-ally hard for you and give you several concepts, because they're motivated to do a good job. You can also post an ad on Craigslist and get several bidders for the job. Ask for portfolios and references if you go that route. There are also graphic design companies, in India, that adver-tise in the U.S., and will do the job for a fraction of the cost.

Website

You must have a website. Your website must be attractive, simple, easy to navigate, and clean. Again, websites can cost you anywhere between $1,000 and $5,000 to build. Follow these steps and you will save tons of money.

1. Choose your URL and hosting.
Go to either www.godaddy.com or www.bluehost.com and enter your business name with .com. Don't bother with any other dot website. Most people will only search .com. Once you find your company name, add it to your cart, for at least two years and at most three years. The site will entice you to buy the .org, .us, .net, etc. Don't do it. It's a waste of your money and if someone else decides to take your exact company name, under .org or .net, and build a website around it, so be it.

When I became an author, I had built my website under my name, Michelle Fondin. After a few years, I knew I was going to redo my entire author site, so I let my website name expire for a couple of months. As far as I know, I'm the only Michelle Fondin in the world with that exact spelling. But when I went to buy my URL again, I found someone had bought it, *my name*. Do you believe it? They didn't built a website around it. But sometimes companies buy expiring website URLs and then try to resell them to you for a profit. So pay attention and don't let your URL expire if you intend on keeping your company open.

Once you've added your URL to the cart, you'll need to purchase hosting. Hosting is so your website can be seen, browsed, and searched once it's up. Generally hosting will cost you anywhere between $10 and $12 per month. You can purchase hosting for the same amount of time that you're buying your URL, that way both will renew at the same time.

Before checkout, they will ask you if you want to add about a million different services. Don't do it. You're running a yoga business, not an online store. You don't need security certificates, protection, or other extras. You need a website that looks pretty, is functional, and will tell your students who you are and where to find you. You don't need a website builder service either. I will teach you how you're going to do that for much less money.

Don't process the payment yet! Look for coupons and promo codes. Both GoDaddy and Bluehost always have promo codes, especially for first time customers. You should get your URL for 99 cents the first year and $10.00 or less the second and third year. Your hosting should be about $240 for two years. Expect to pay around $250 to $275 during this transaction.

2. Select a template.

WordPress is the best way to build and maintain a website. I cannot recommend it enough. The first two times I had websites built, they were custom made and it was a pain in my butt. Here's why. In order to change anything on the website I had to contact the designers. In my case, the designers were my sister and boyfriend respectively. But that still meant I was bothering someone and taking up their time. If you hire a designer, you'll be paying at least $50 for every change. Your website will change all the time, so you could rack up quite a bill with your web designer. You'll add blog posts, schedule changes, add classes and workshops, and hopefully add teachers. You need to have the power to change your website often and on your own.

The WordPress format is a community-based open website forum. There are free templates, but they have minimal functionality and are very basic. The least expensive template site I've found is www.themeforest.com. When you go to this site, search WordPress templates and you can enter the keywords *yoga* or *spa*. Generally, you can expect to pay between $29 and $59 for a good template. If you are going to hire a designer to help you get started, ask him or her if the template you are about to buy is good and functional. Also, look at the reviews for the template you like. Most templates from

Theme Forest come with six months of support from the authors and that's really all you need. Once you purchase your template, download it right away.

3. Installing your template and theme.

Call your hosting company and ask to talk to hosting technical support. Tell them you'd like to install a Word-Press theme on a URL and hosting you just purchased. They will talk your through first installing WordPress and then the template theme to your site. If the person on the line can't help you, ask for someone else. Be persistent. They will help.

4. Building your site.

You can build your site on WordPress with relative ease. But if you're new to website building it can be time consuming and frustrating. My suggestion is to have a designer build the initial pages for you and then you can make content and image changes as needed. Again, you don't have to pay $1,500 to have a designer build pages on a WordPress theme. Your template has done that for you. Pay a college student $200 to $300 to do it.

Last summer I had six high school and college interns. Two of my interns, seventeen-year-olds, built my author website and it looks awesome. Go to www.michellefondinauthor.com to check it out. Motivated teenagers and young adults often do a better job than adults who are busy with a lot of different clients.

5. Photos and images

Visuals are really important for a website. You want it to pop and look beautiful. Make sure to add a nice picture of you with a great bio. Have a friend do a photo shoot with you to get some great pics. For the other images on your site, get high quality stock photos. Go to www.photodune.com to get low cost stock images. They will cost you about $5 to $9 per image. For each webpage include at least three images.

Don't try to download free images on the Internet. It's not worth it. Most images are protected under copyright laws and they will find you.

6. Widgets and plugins

Since WordPress is community-based, it has thousands of widgets and plugins to make your website functional. You can choose from calendars, social media widgets, shopping carts, and integrated banners. Most of them are free. You can ask your website designer to search these if you have an idea for a key feature you'd like to include in your website.

7. Browse other yoga business websites.

Look through at least twenty yoga studio and yoga business websites to get ideas and see what you like and don't like. Many yoga studios near me have mediocre websites that are difficult to navigate. The customer decides in about 15 seconds if he or she will stay on your website or not. You want to learn what works. What elements hold your attention on a site? Use those elements to build your site.

Payment processing

Before marketing your classes, you need a way for your students to pay you. Even though it will cost you a little more in processing fees, go simpler rather than fancier. In the beginning, I got caught up with merchant processing agreements that ultimately cost me a lot of money. Besides cash and check, have two methods of taking credit cards.

1. PayPal

The easiest way to accept credit card payment is through PayPal. The processing fee is 2.9% + $0.30 per transaction. Two point nine might not seem like a lot but it adds up. Yet, a lot of customers like to use PayPal, so have that option open.

2. Square

Square allows you to be able to swipe credit cards or enter them into a chip reader device. The advantage to using Square is that there is no monthly service fee or minimum transactions per month. Square's magnetic reader is free and their chip reader is $49 as a one-time fee. You want to swipe a card for your protection against fraud and you will also pay less in fees. Square's swipe fee is 2.75% and if you key in a card it's 3.5% plus a 15 cent transaction fee. You can set up your items and store on your phone or iPad. The website for Square is www. squareup.com.

3. MINDBODY

Most yoga studios use MINDBODY business management software because of its functionality. It's very advanced and has many functions including payment processing, client scheduling, reminders, scheduling classes, workshops, and courses, staffing, accounting, and more. I used MINDBODY for several years while running my yoga studio and was pleased with it. However, it did get extremely expensive. The pro version costs $125 per month. With that, you are also paying a monthly merchant processing fee of fifteen dollars, plus 2.75% for qualified payments and 3.5% + $0.15 for non-qualified payments. It gets expensive really fast.

After I took my yoga business home, I discovered that the MINDBODY subscription, plus all of the fees, cost me 17% of my income just to book classes. It was an insane choice for me to stay. So I opted for a new choice, with less bells and whistles, but one that still works.

4. Pocket Suite

The idea of Pocket Suite is to run your business on your phone with its app. At first, it took some getting used to, but now I'm a pro at it. The developers are nice and accommodating. You can use the app with minimum functionality for free and if you want to buy the subscription, it's $19.99 per month.

With Pocket Suite you can create classes, workshops, book appointments, have customers make payments, and track your income for the month. The processing fee is only 2.5%.

Email Blaster Service

In order to run a business, you need to build your customer list. Once you have a customer list, you need to keep in touch with them. The easiest and most efficient way is to send out newsletters, interesting articles, YouTube videos, and information on upcoming classes or workshops. You can do this through email blaster services. I personally use Constant Contact. Another service is Mail Chimp.

You can try Constant Contact for free for 60 days. After your trial runs out, you pay per amount of clients. With zero to 500 contacts, you pay $20 per month. If you have over 500 contacts, but under 2,500, you pay $45 per month and so on. They also have prepaid plans so you can save money. Go to www.constantcontact.com.

Mail Chimp is less costly than Constant Contact. They have a free account where you can have up to 2,000 contacts. Their professional account is $10 per month. I'm less familiar with the functionality of Mail Chimp. But I know a lot of businesses use this service. Go to www.mailchimp.com.

The advantages of using an email marketing software service are many. Both of these services are permission-based, meaning that you must have implied or express permission to send out emails to your contacts. There are anti-spam laws that could get you in trouble if you start sending emails out to people who never showed an interest in your business. But if a potential client fills out a card at your business to get more information, he or she has given implied permission. Even if a client registers on your site to sign up for classes, but doesn't follow through, that is still implied permission. Express permission is when the client signs up through a sign up box on your website or via newsletter that was forwarded by another client. Both of these services also have a "safe unsubscribe" button so that contacts who don't want your emails anymore can unsubscribe from your list.

Another advantage is that you get to keep all the pretty emails you've already created in your account. To send a similar email, all you need to do is copy and paste into a new email campaign and make changes. You also get to see your email campaign statistics. You will know how many contacts opened the emails, which ones clicked through, and who didn't open them.

You can also automate emails to send them out on certain days and times. For example, you can create a series of emails, in a single day, to go out over the next two weeks.

Both Constant Contact and Mail Chimp have opt-in sign up forms you can put on your website. This is a must-have. With WordPress, you can easily integrate your sign up form. And when a potential client signs up, it goes directly to the contact, list that you choose, on your email software account.

Finally, here's note of caution for these must-haves. It can be tempting to ask a willing family member or friend for help with some of these business necessities. My advice to you is, don't do it unless you are completely broke. I have had family members and a boyfriend help me. Since they both had other jobs, my job didn't take priority. Their work was fantastic, but I felt bad for not paying them. So when your work gets delayed and you start to get annoyed, it can ruin family relationships and friendships. Also, if you don't like the design concepts or work, you might not feel like being honest for fear that you might hurt his or her feelings. Then, you have a logo, website, or brand identity that you don't love. However, if you're willing to pay a family member or friend the going rate, go ahead. You have every right to make the same demands as any other client, because you're paying for the same service. I have a working relationship with my son who's a designer. I hire him to do my book covers, including the cover for this book, but I pay him what he asks. Plus, we have an honest enough relationship that if I don't like something I'll tell him. And if he thinks my work isn't up to par, he'll tell me.

Free Marketing

There are many different ways you can market your classes without spending a dime. Remember that marketing is all about building relationships and creating trust. You want your target audience to become familiar with who you are and what you do. Then, you want to build a rapport, and finally, you want your audience to trust your brand.

The Internet makes free marketing easy if you do things right. With a creative mindset, you can think up loads of ideas to market for free.

Social media marketing

Using social media for marketing and building an audience is a great way to allow people to get to know you.

It takes time to build up a following on social media, but it's worth it. It helps build your reputation as an expert in your field.

Thinking of your target audience, start business pages on the appropriate social media sites. As teens and young adults tell me, Facebook is only for old people. To them, old people are over 35 years old. Twitter is pretty much for everyone, but doesn't necessarily work well for a yoga business. YouTube is great if you like to create videos. Instagram seems to work well to get a big following and is more youth oriented. You want your social media business pages to reflect your brand across the board. Even though the toppers are different sizes, have your brand designer create one for Facebook, Twitter, and YouTube.

Try not to use your personal social media pages for business. You will annoy your family and friends. From time to time it's okay to post something, but use your business pages for frequent posting. You can, however, ask your family and friends to like your business pages or follow you. The ones who are interested will follow.

Post to social media frequently, like two to three times per day. The rule of thumb in social media posting is, 80% of the content you post should be other people's relevant material and 20% is your original content. You don't want your clients to feel you're constantly selling. You are there to solve their problems and pain. Reposting is easy if you have a few favorite sites such as Yoga Journal, Yoga Alliance, or a social media account with inspirational quotes. Search out the latest news on yoga, meditation, or alternative health on reputable sites and post those articles.

There are services that can help you queue up posts so you don't have to think about it daily. I use Buffer (www.buffer.com) to queue up my social media posts. Buffer has a free version or you can subscribe. I used the free version for a while and it worked just fine. You get statistics on your social media posts, which is great. You can also repost past posts that did well.

Here is one last important thing to note in the world of social media. As a business owner, you are now a public figure. Like it or not, you need to protect your brand and reputation. Be extremely careful about what you post on your personal social media pages. Your clients, past, present, and future, will always be watching you at some point. I have tons of former clients who still read my stuff even though they haven't taken classes with me in years. Your integrity should be seamless. You need to be the same person online that you are offline. Even if you're just joking, be careful about what you say, what you post, what you repost, and what you comment on. People will constantly be looking for inconsistencies in your character. That's just the nature of how business works.

Let me tell you a story. In France, in 2006, before I started teaching yoga, I had a yoga teacher whom I really respected. She was a great teacher and embodied all of the qualities I hoped to emulate as a yoga teacher. She organized a weekend yoga retreat and of course I signed up to go. Before the retreat, she kept talking about this teacher friend that she loved and respected. She said she had invited this friend to the retreat to talk about the Alexander Technique. My teacher had built up such a huge expectation around this other woman that I was anxious to meet her. When I finally did get to meet her, I saw a depressed looking overweight woman who drank loads of wine throughout a four-hour dinner. It wasn't at all what I had expected. This woman was not an inspiration of health. After that, it made me lose respect for my yoga teacher. Why? Because there were holes in her story. The woman, she had invited to the yoga retreat, did not represent a person who emulated health and wellbeing. She didn't seem like an amazing person. She appeared, in every way, to be a sad, old, out of shape woman with a drinking problem.

I'm not saying this to be cynical or disrespectful. I'm telling you this to show you that what you do and how you live your life shows through in everything. You must be consistent in thought, word, and action each and every time.

YouTube videos

Videos are a great way for a yoga teacher to show off what he or she knows. You can do a whole lot with video to help develop a sense of trust between you and your potential clients. People today are more visual than ever and they don't take the time necessary to read content. Try to have a video on every single page on your website introducing your service or have a sample video of you teaching a few yoga poses. Get your students to fall in love with you before they even meet you.

Search Engine Optimization (SEO)

If you know nothing about search engine optimization, learn quickly or get a web master who can do it for you. WordPress has plugins for SEO and many of them are free. Search engine optimization is so that search engines such as Google, Safari, or Bing can find your website. When potential clients do a search such as "yoga in my area", the search engine looks for keywords linked to websites. On each page of your website, you're going to add keywords so people can find you. On the backend of your WordPress site, go to "plugins" and click on the button "add a new plugin". You can enter "SEO" in the search bar to come up with the top plugins for SEO. Once you install your plugin, you can go to each page of your website and enter the appropriate information such as your page keyword, meta data, and other keywords associated with your page. Without adding SEO keywords, your website is basically useless to search engines.

Blog posts

The beautiful thing about WordPress is that it started out as a website builder for bloggers, so most WordPress sites have blog pages. A great way to attract new students to your website and your business is to start a blog. If you decide to do a blog, make sure you're consistent. Write one or two posts per month and send them out to your mailing list and post them on social media. It's free and another way you can build trust with your audience.

Networking meetings

Business networking meetings are not necessarily a great way to get business, but a great way to meet other business owners and hopefully gain clients through referral. In the beginning, I attended a few networking meetings regularly and even started one of my own. Being an entrepreneur can be a lonely endeavor and sometimes it can help to be pumped up by others who are in the same boat.

Early on I found my yoga studio space through a networking meeting. I also found my first Ayurvedic client ever. Again, networking is also about building relationships.

Meetup groups

I love Meetup.com. I have found many groups of interest and met a lot interesting people. Join groups in the arena of health and wellness. Don't go to Meetups to directly sell or pitch your business. But as you're getting to know people, mention what you do and see if people ask questions. You can also start a yoga Meetup. It's not free to use the Meetup website, but you can charge members for each Meetup. Or if you prefer to offer a free yoga class or guided meditation, you can ask members to give a one-time donation of $5 to cover the cost of the site.

Review websites

Getting good reviews are the best way to generate new business. When you're searching for a good restaurant, don't you look at the reviews first?

People are consistently busy, so the only way you're going to get reviews is if you ask. The two main sites where people look at reviews for yoga are Yelp and Google. I'm not a big fan of Yelp, although a lot of people go there for reviews. Yelp has an automated bot that filters out reviews, mostly good ones. If your yoga student is a new user to Yelp or has only used Yelp a couple of times, the Yelp bot will think it's a fraudulent review and filter it out. When I was starting out I was getting reviews, but

90% of my reviews on Yelp were filtered out. It was frustrating. When I called Yelp to complain, they said their bot was foolproof. One day, my sister, who lives in Chicago, was in town for a visit. She came to my yoga studio to take a class and left a review on Yelp. Of course she gave a good review because she's my sister. Even though Yelp claims that they remove fraudulent reviews and keep the real ones, at one time, my sister's review was the only one not filtered out. Although her review wasn't downright fraudulent, it was a bit of a conflict of interest. *So much for Yelp's foolproof bot.* I'm told that Yelp wants you, as a business owner, to pay for monthly advertising with them. The last time they pitched me, it was upwards of $300 per month. When you pay that monthly fee, somehow the Yelp bot gets friendlier and you get to keep more of your good reviews. Anyway, it's your call. My advice to you is to not lock yourself into any monthly advertising until you've exhausted your free options for a while.

That being said; go ahead and create your business page on Yelp. If you don't, someone else will. Users can add a business to Yelp and leave a review without your knowledge, so you better beat them to it and make it pretty. Creating your business page on Yelp is free. You can add a description, a link to your website, directions to your studio, and photos.

Create a Google plus page for your business. Add a nice description and pretty pictures. Once you do and get it verified by Google, your students can start leaving reviews. Since Google is the number one search engine, these reviews, happily, will show up first.

One last thing about reviews. If you get a bad review, that you believe is unjust, answer the review on the public website. There is often a feature where you can respond to a review. But keep your response positive and customer service oriented.

Ask for referrals

Referrals are the best way to gain new business and they're free to acquire. When you have great clients, ask them flat out for referrals. Say, "Do you have any friends or family members who might want to try my classes?" I have one exception for the "no free class" rule and that is for referrals. If a student asks me, "Can I bring my husband to try out a class for free?" I always say, "Yes". Your raving fans will always refer other people to you, but you need to ask.

Referrals can also come from other people, who have never been to your yoga classes, but are people with whom you've built a rapport. When I started teaching prenatal yoga, I gave out my brochures to all of the OB/Gyns in the area. Every couple of months I would give more brochures. And guess what happened? I became known as the prenatal yoga expert in my area. Many OB/Gyns, who had never even met me, were referring patients to my classes. Then, the nurses would call me when they were running low on brochures. Those were the best referrals I have ever gotten.

Free events

I am not a fan of free events, but in the beginning you can try them. When I started teaching I would do free events from time to time. More often than not, I would have one or two people show up. Most people don't value free. If it's free, they think something's up. I've talked to many other business owners who have had the same experience.

Another version of a free event, you can do to generate more interest, is to hold a donation event for a local charity. Let's suppose you're starting out and your audience is comprised of young couples. You could hold a fun partner class with an optional donation for a local food bank or women's shelter. I've been to a Tibetan bowl meditation where they post a sign at the door that says, "Suggested donation $15-$25". That way students know the value of the class they're about to take.

Flyers in busy places

Creating flyers will cost you the price of paper and ink and might not generate a whole lot of interest, but could get you one or two clients. I've gotten business from posting flyers at local coffee houses and grocery stores. Make your flyer interesting and allow it to stand out. Capitalize on your area of expertise. If you like working with children, one class I've consistently gotten demands for is yoga for kids. I've done one class session and it was successful. But since most of my evening and weekend classes are for adults, I couldn't find a time slot that would accommodate both kids in school and working parents. However, if you post flyers for a kids' yoga class, you're likely to get some calls.

Practice give, give, get

Early in my writing career I learned from my publicist, Steve Harrison, to look at marketing as dating. You would never go up to a new guy or gal and say, "Hey, do you want to marry me?" *Well, maybe you would, but that would be creepy.* Instead, you would say, "Hey, would you like to go get a cup of coffee sometime. I'd like to get to know you better." The same goes for client acquisition. Many sales people do the equivalent of a marriage proposal. They say, "I'm selling this. Do you want to buy it?"

Steve taught me the "Give, Give, Get" principle. You want to give twice before you receive. For example, give your prospective client a 50% discount on the first yoga class. Then, send out a free video you made on how to correctly perform five yoga asanas. Finally, ask them how they liked the class and video and then ask if they'd like to begin with a starter yoga package.

Once you start implementing all of the free marketing ideas, you'll start to generate business, rest assured. It sounds like a lot of work and it is, but it will pay off big time.

Paid Marketing

At times, you will find it necessary to use paid marketing, especially if you open a studio. I'm going to sort through the types of paid marketing I've used and let you know if they're good or a waste of money. When in doubt, be frugal. Your marketing dollars can fly away from you faster than you realize.

Deal-of-the-day coupons such as Groupon or Living Social

I owe much of my success to Groupon. Using Groupon and Living Social were a blessing and a curse. Deal-of-the-day coupons are the best way to grow your business fast. The problem is that it can become addicting. Cash flow is often a problem when you're starting a business and these companies almost guarantee you income. Yoga class vouchers are very popular on Groupon. The problem is that they are offered at a deep discount and many of the clients aren't looking for a home studio, they're looking for a deal. Another problem is that a lot of clients don't read the fine print and buy two or more vouchers when the deal explicitly says "one per customer".

But all in all, I acquired many clients through these deals. However, you have to be smart about it.

1. Negotiate your deal well with the company.

Traditionally, Groupon will get 50% of each deal that is already marked 50% off. So if you offer a 5-class package for $25, they take $12.50. When you're on the phone with your representative, negotiate the share. Before Groupon went public, I negotiated a deal that was 37% for Groupon and 63% for me with no credit card processing fees.

2. Only offer what you're willing to sell.

Don't go broke getting a voucher deal. Offer two small deals like 5 and 10 classes and cap it at a low number, for example, 100 vouchers total. When they sell out, they sell out. Then, wait another six months before offering another deal. Here's what happened with me. I ran a deal for a long time and ended up competing with myself. In other words, Groupon and other deal-of-the-day companies have more marketing dollars than you have, so they come up first on search engines. So when a new client would look me up, they would see the Groupon deal before my actual website. As a result, I was taking away full paying clients from myself.

3. Have a special offer ready for your Groupon client before his or her voucher runs out.
By the second lesson, take your client aside and ask him or her for feedback on the classes. Then, offer a deal the client can't refuse. I used to offer a $99 per month unlimited class special with the option to buy up to six months. As it turned out, it wasn't a great deal for me, but it was great for the client. Make sure your offer is competitive, but also one that doesn't put you in the poor house.

4. Have a plan as to how you're going to handle customers who don't follow the rules.
With deal-of-the-day specials, some customers will break the rules. You need to have a plan. A client will come in a day after the voucher expires. Or a client will have bought five vouchers and complain that now Groupon will not refund their money, because they bought them with three different accounts and three different credit cards. I know I'm making this out to be the biggest hassle in the world, but it's not. I'm simply trying to help you cover all your bases before you go through with a voucher deal.

All in all this paid marketing is the only one that guarantees you customers who will walk in your door and it's rather brilliant.

Pay-Per-Click Ads

Every website imaginable has pay-per-click ads. If you're smart, they work, but it's almost like putting money in a slot machine and watching it go away. You get a little reward, then you pay a lot of money and get another little reward. And so it goes.

Let me tell you this upfront. I spent way too much money on Google Ad Words trying to outbid my competitors. Again, it was a bad move. You can also screw yourself by paying too much money for Google Ads. The reason, that took me way too long to figure out, is that when you pay for an ad on Google, you do get prime real estate, either up top or on the side up top. However, if a client searches your name or your business name, or even "yoga in your city" and you come up number one, two, or three, your Google Ad will also come up. But the ad will come up way at the top. And guess what? The person doing the search will, nine times out of ten, click on the ad instead of your direct website link because it's the most prominent. So you get charged for the click even though your website showed up just one or two lines down.

One way to remedy this is to cap your daily spending. Another way is to select keywords that have nothing to do with your name, your business name, or anything that pertains to you personally. You want to select keywords that only pertain to your services or offerings.

Facebook ads have never worked for me to gain clients. The concept is great, since Facebook has very targeted pay-per-click ads, but they are also very expensive. The most that I got through paid Facebook ads were "likes" on my business page.

With that knowledge, try both and see how they work for you. Start with a small budget, like a dollar or two per day. Most of all, when you get customers, ask them where they found you. That way you can track your marketing dollars to see what works.

Health fairs and yoga fairs

Over the years I've done many health and yoga fairs. I don't find they're a good return on investment. Getting a table at a yoga fair is expensive, even if you share with another vendor and it's difficult to get clients through these events. Think about it. You've been to a fair or expo of some sort, right? You walk through the fair, stopping at booths, maybe taking flyers and brochures, or maybe not. You're looking at art, clothes, you're getting a massage demonstration, and tasting the latest power bar. Then, you get hungry, go for some food, get tired, and go home. The bag, with all the flyers and brochures, either sits in the back of your car for six months, or gets buried on your kitchen table. You never look through them. You forget who you even saw or talked to at the fair, because now everything is a blur. *Does that sound familiar? Oh I know it does. Go clean out all of those old flyers. No, wait, don't go! Keep reading.*

Often, the reason I did them was because I was invited by various companies to partake in their employee health fairs and I didn't have to pay a booth fee. But it was a waste of an entire afternoon, because I never got any clients. Each time I thought it might be different, but it wasn't.

The few times I did yoga fairs, I did so because another studio owner was running them and I liked her.

But besides selling some Ayurvedic products and a few books, I never made a profit. I just broke even.

Subscription marketing services

I have been pitched by dozens of subscription marketing services and have tried a couple. My advice to you is don't do it. One was called Demandforce. It's extremely expensive for what it is and you get locked into a year contract. What some of these services try to do is integrate automated email marketing, social media marketing, and reviews all into one. Here's the problem. You can get many of these services for free and do an even better job. Plus the reviews they acquire for you, from your own clients, are available only through their website when you pay. Once you stop your subscription with the service, your reviews disappear.

A final word about paid marketing. When you're a new company, it seems that everyone has his or her hands in your pocket. *Ew gross, right? Unless it's Zac Efron, he can put his hands in...Oh shoot, sorry, back to the topic.* As soon as you incorporate or get your URL, you will get dozens of calls daily from people who just "want to help". If you're eager to get your business off the ground, it can seem tempting. Hold back and try all of these marketing tips, but not all at once. *You're running a marathon, not a sprint here. Do a little leg work and you'll see results.*

Recap on Lessons Learned: Marketing

1. Market is not about selling; it's about relationship building.

2. Pinpoint your target market and find out everything you can about them.

3. Make a list of the marketing must-haves and do one or two per day until you get them done.

4. Explore the free marketing ideas and see which ones appeal to you.

5. Start networking. Talk with other business owners and find out what marketing works best for them.

CHAPTER SIX

Your Business Model

BEFORE YOU TEACH YOUR first class, reflect upon what you'd like for your business. How do you see it one year down the road? Two years? Five years? Do you want to see it grow exponentially or do you want to keep it small and intimate? Do you want to rent a space or teach out of your home? The answers to these questions will largely determine your business model.

Your Legal Status

Depending on your business outcome, you'll need to establish the legal status for your business. This is important on many levels. For accounting purposes, you'll want to keep your personal finances and business finances separate. When you apply for a business credit card, you'll want a tax ID number instead of using your personal social security number. For tax purposes, you may want to become an employee of your business and pay other employees. To protect your assets, should you get sued or go bankrupt, your legal status will matter. For all of those reasons and more, it's important to choose your legal status now.

Sole proprietor

Being a sole proprietor is the same as being self-employed. Another term for sole proprietor is "Doing Business As" or DBA. When you're a sole proprietor, there are no separate papers to fill out. You are yourself, working for yourself. The definition of sole proprietor is one person. As soon as you have two or more people running a business, you can't use this legal business status.

As a sole proprietor, you use your social security number and file taxes under your name. Since you'll be generating income, you will fill out a Schedule C on your 1040 tax form. Through your Schedule C, you'll be able to deduct your expenses for running your business and also deduct money paid to contractors to whom you gave a 1099-MISC.

The selection of Sole Proprietor does not protect you or your assets. If you lose all of your money running your business or if you charge up all of your credit cards, your debtors go after you and your assets.

You may, however, need to register your business name with your city or county and pay a small tax. Check with your city or county about the rules of sole proprietorships.

LLC or Limited Liability Company

The next step up from being a Sole Proprietor is defining your business as a limited liability company (LLC). A limited liability company is an association of one or more members. It's not an incorporated entity. The advantages of an LLC are that you can still file your individual taxes and include your company on your personal taxes. Owners of an LLC do not need to be U.S. Citizens or permanent residents. You will have limited liability for business debts and obligations. You will also have more credibility in the eyes of lenders, suppliers, and partners when you form an LLC.

There are, however, downsides to an LLC. You can't issue stocks so you might not attract potential investors. LLCs are not subject the same laws in every state. And you may be subject to self-employment tax.

C Corporation

As a yoga business owner, forming and maintaining a C corporation is probably not going to be the best choice. Most big businesses, in the United States, are C corporations because there is unlimited potential for growth. You can create an unlimited amount of stocks and also have an unlimited number of stockholders. However, if you want to create an S Corporation, you must first incorporate your company as a C Corporation. Then, fill out a form to create a Pass-Through Entity to give it an S Corporation status.

S Corporation

An S Corporation election will give you most of the same benefits as a C Corporation, but will give you added advantages if you remain a small company. Both C and S corporations give you limited liability like an LLC.

Just like a C corporation, you will need to file Articles of Incorporation, have shareholders, directors, and officers. C corporations are subject to double taxes. The corporation is taxed once and the shareholders are taxed when they receive dividends. An S corporation is only taxed once. Another advantage of an S corporation is that they are only required to file taxes once yearly, whereas C corporations must file quarterly. S corporations are limited to 100 shareholders, which, again, should not be problem for a yoga business.

My business, The Ayurvedic Path, ran as an S corporation under the advice of my sister. The advantages were the limited liability and being able to deduct my health-care costs as an employee of the corporation.

Choosing the legal status right for your company

When you're starting out, there is nothing wrong with being a sole proprietor unless you're opening a yoga studio in a rented space. However, it's more advantageous for financial reasons to have either an LLC or an S corporation. You'll want to open up a separate bank account for your business and to do that you'll need a separate tax identification number. If you love your company name, you'll want to claim and register the name with the State Corporation Commission, Secretary of State, or whatever governing body takes care of incorporation in your state. If you know you'll hire employees for your business, start off with an S corporation rather than an LLC. You can also become an employee of your company and avoid the self-employment tax.

How to form an LLC or S Corporation

If you do a quick Internet search, you'll find plenty of third party companies who will gladly take you through the steps of forming your LLC or corporation for a fee. My advice to you is to do it yourself. I was able to quickly figure it out and I had no business experience whatsoever. If I did it, you can too.

Step one: Choose a legal name and reserve it. When you call the appropriate governing body, you can do a quick name search to see if it's been taken in your state. You can reserve your company name and it should cost you no more than $10. Next, request your tax identification number. Go to https://www.irs.gov/businesses/small-businesses-self-employed/apply-for-an-employer-identification-number-ein-online to apply for your Employer Identification Number (EIN). It's free to apply and get your EIN number with the IRS. Don't pay a third party for this service. It will take you no more than 15 minutes to apply online.

If you're not sure who incorporates in your state, go to the local chamber of commerce to get information on where you would go. In Virginia, where I live, it's called the State Corporation Commission. The website will be a .gov website. Don't get tricked with similar names. If your search takes you to a .com, it's a third party company.

Step two: Draft and file your Articles of Organization for an LLC or Articles of Incorporation for a C or S corporation with the appropriate governing body. You can expect to pay around $100 to file a new company.

Step three: Decide on the owners, who will run the business, and who holds other roles. If you have a business partner, decide on the percentage of ownership. If you have a C corporation with S election, you'll need a director, officer, and shareholder. In the beginning, if you're the only one, you can hold all of these roles.

Step four: Apply for business licenses and other certificates if needed. If you're teaching yoga at various locations, you won't need a business license. Once you have a brick and mortar establishment, you'll need to go to the city hall associated with the location of your studio to obtain your business license.

Step five: For an S election for your C Corporation, you need to file Form 2553, Election by a Small Business Corporation, (https://www.irs.gov/pub/irs-pdf/f2553.pdf) with the IRS within 60 days of incorporating your C Corporation.

> Whew! You made it! I know your brain is hurting now from all of this business jargon. Get up, do some stretches. Shake your booty out of that chair. Eat some chocolate and get ready for the next big step.

Modeling: Learning from Successful Yoga Businesses Around You

One major step I skipped and one that I'm urging you to take seriously is the concept of modeling. Like one of my favorite teachers, Tony Robbins, teaches, "Success leaves clues." Look for these clues in other yoga businesses before you start. As my mother used to say, "Steal with your eyes."

Do this homework and you'll be well ahead of your competition.

Go visit and take classes at no less than ten yoga studios in your area. Even if those studios teach styles of yoga, that are not your cup of tea, go anyway. Take a least two drop-in classes at each studio. Study everything about these studios. Analyze their websites before you visit. Don't book online, call and book your first class. Listen to how the person, who picks up the phone, treats you. Did a person pick up the phone? Did you leave a message? Did you get a call back right away? Analyze the parking situation. How does the studio feel when you walk in the front door? What is the vibe? Do they have a front desk? How do they greet you? Arrive a few minutes early to class and talk to the students before the session starts. Tell them you're new and would like to know what they enjoy about the studio. Ask them which teachers are the best and why. If you get a lot of information and can't remember it all, run to the bathroom and write it down. Remember, you're playing the role of detective to get to the bottom of the best yoga business practices. Make a list of what works and what doesn't work.

If you're feeling really bold, ask the studio owner if you could take him or her out to tea or coffee to ask some business advice. Ask the owner what tends to work in your area. Every location is different. For example, I wanted to teach a senior yoga class at my studio. I wasn't getting any registrations and found out that, two miles down the road, the YMCA was offering free yoga classes to seniors. Of course they wouldn't pay me for class, when around the corner they could get it for free.

Don't try to pave your own way, model success.

Your Business Philosophy

You've chosen your business name and have your legal status. You have a list of business practices, from successful yoga businesses, that you'd like to model. Now you need to decide on your business philosophy. Your business philosophy will determine the vibe of your yoga business. It will include your mission statement, business vision, and corporate culture. It's really important that you reflect upon this and give it serious consideration.

This will be especially important as you begin to hire other yoga teachers or employees to help you. You will need to make sure they share your vision.

For example, I had a personal philosophy that became a business philosophy regarding the cleanliness of my studio. I had been to a number of gyms who had dirty and broken down equipment. I made the decision early on that my studio would be impeccable. It would smell nice. The mats would be clean and odor free. The bathrooms would be perfect. I started with the practice myself. I would arrive twenty minutes before class and make sure the studio was in perfect shape. I would also stay twenty minutes after to make sure the studio was perfect for the next class or the next day. Then, I taught my clients to respect the equipment and told them where everything went. When I hired teachers, I shared with them the priority of an impeccable studio and gave them the job to make sure it was perfect before and after class. If a mat got a little worn out, I would replace it immediately. Clients noticed this and commented on how refreshing it was to have a pretty and impeccably clean studio 100% of the time.

We also respected our clients' time. We would start classes on time and end on time. I learned this trait from my lead teacher at the Chopra Center, who pounded this principle into our minds before graduation. Punctuality is about respect. Everyone, who worked for me, knew this was one of our business practices.

We also greeted every single student by name as they came in the door. If we didn't know the name, we would ask. But I made it a practice to study the roster and pre-registrations before class and memorize the names on the list. If I saw two new students on the roster and the names were Tracey and Srivanthi, I could assume that Srivanthi might be East Indian. So when a new East Indian woman walked in, I could say, "Srivanthi?" and be almost 100% accurate.

Do you see that if you have set principles and a business philosophy, you will be able to grow your business with a set direction? If you don't have that set in place, your business will be chaotic and incongruent.

Your Business Plan

Unless you're borrowing money or you have a business partner, you can make a simple business plan to project what your business will look like one to five years down the road. If you're borrowing money, signing a lease agreement for a costly space, and/ or have a business partner, you need an elaborate business plan in place.

You can find many free business plan templates online. Take some time now and fill out your business plan.

Who Will Help?

Even if you're a sole proprietor, you'll need help running your business. Don't be a lone ranger like I was. You'll crash and burn. *Let's set the record straight right now. You are Superman or Superwoman. However, even superheroes have helpers.*

There are so many things you'll need to do as a business owner and a limited amount of hours in the day. Something will have to give. Here is a list of tasks and positions you could possibly hire out or get family to do:

- Housekeeping for your home
- Gardening for your home
- Housekeeping for your studio
- Accounting
- Website upkeep
- Social media posting
- Personal assistant or admin
- Babysitter
- Cook
- Networker
- Flyer distributor
- Graphic designer

Before the dollar signs start adding up in your head, let's think outside of the box. There are two sub-groups you could hire for a minimal amount of money: teenagers or young adults and senior citizens. Teens are great because many of them are looking for experience to add to a resume or college application. This past summer I hired, for free, six high school and college interns. In exchange, I offered to help them with college application essays. I also fed them snacks when they were working and treated them to an occasional ice cream or pizza. Retired seniors are great because sometimes they're just looking for part-time work. They have life experience and are usually really responsible. You can pay minimum wage and know that they won't have the distractions that a younger worker might have.

If you have kids, make them do more. Kids are too entitled in today's world anyway. Didn't you do more work around the house when you were a kid than your kids do? Over the years I've saddled my kids with loads of busy work. They've put stamps on envelopes, looked up corporations I could pitch for corporate yoga, put stickers on brochures, and rolled up yoga mats. And did I pay them? No. I didn't pay them when they were young. They needed to be grateful for having a mom who was working and paying the bills. As they got older I would pay them something. It depended on the child's personality too. My son Jay is a master negotiator. So when he was sixteen, I started paying him $10 per hour for various tasks. But he only worked a couple of hours weekly. Now that he's a college graduate, he sets his own prices and gets more money. Having your children work for you builds character and teaches them the intensity of running a business. Plus, it makes them feel valued and that they're a part of something. Don't get me wrong. My kids have never done yoga and don't show any interest in ever doing it. But they have learned about the business end of yoga.

Your Services and Products

Decide what services and products you'll provide to your clients. Start with a limited number of class offerings and see what works. Some yoga teachers are also Reiki masters, massage therapists, psychics, jewelry makers, or crystal sellers. So when you ask them what they do, they answer, "I do a lot of things." Then they rattle off the list. It's so confusing that you don't even know what they're good at.

I was at a networking meeting where I met this woman whose elevator pitch was about babies being tongue-tied. I thought she was a surgeon or speech therapist. As it turns out, she was referring to her service of myofascial release massage. In addition to having no idea what that was, I was also confused as to what she was trying to sell. We were all adults at the meeting and business owners, so it wasn't clear whom she was trying to pitch. When I finally sat down to talk with her, I realized she was a fascinating woman who specialized in way too many things. But as I listened to her, I learned that her real specialty was working with pregnant women for doula services, prenatal massage, and hypnobirthing classes. Yet if you look at her business brochure, it's really very confusing.

While many yoga teachers also have other services they provide, you need to focus on one or two so you don't confuse clients. They need to quickly know what you offer.

When I started The Ayurvedic Path, I offered three services: yoga, meditation, and Ayurveda. In each of these categories I offered several different services. But if you looked at my website, you saw a header for yoga, meditation, and Ayurveda. If you add more than three, you'll really start the confusion.

As far as products go, you'll need to assess if it's profitable for you. Unless you're an artist carrying your own artwork such as paintings, jewelry, or clothing, carrying stock is a huge hassle. I carried stock on Ayurvedic products, but didn't make much money on them. It was truly more of a pain in the butt than anything else.

Write down everything you do well and focus on your top two or three. All of your marketing efforts will go into letting your strengths shine.

The Power of Focus

Many businesses fail because the owners lack focus. They try to do too many things and have too many innovative ideas. Look at the most successful businesses in the Fortune 500. Apple has a limited number of products, but work their products to perfection. Tesla has three different car models and now sells home solar panels.

What often happens, when you're an entrepreneur building a new business, is that you let fear dominate you. And that never works out to your best interest. You want to stand out from the crowd, be original, innovative, and cutting edge. You decide that your yoga studio will be a studio space, bookstore, juice bar, and hang out place. So you do a little bit of everything and try in earnest to run it all.

Another enemy of focus is lack of time management. For example, you put all of your focus on acquiring new customers that you forget your current ones. Or you put a lot of effort into teaching, but forget to have more customers in the pipeline.

A frequent problem, when you're wearing many hats, is constant multitasking. For example, you're preparing your yoga class plan, then the phone rings and you're answering the call, then you get an important email, so you answer that, then you get a text, and so on.

When you're focused, you'll get more done. As you're planning your day, allocate a time for each activity. Set two times a day to check and answer emails. Answer texts at the top of the hour for five minutes. Let the phone go to voicemail if you're preparing for class. Discipline yourself to have those set times so you can be more focused and efficient.

Start Small & Keep It Simple

You can always do more. Have you ever cooked a recipe you were excited about and realized afterward you added too much salt or hot pepper? Once the recipe is made, you can't take out those ingredients. But if you realize your food is too bland, you can always add more. The same is true in business. Yes, you will get discounts for adding more, but maybe you don't want or need more. In the following categories, you might want to save your money and time by testing the waters before going all out.

Promotional materials

It can be exhilarating when you're creating your first business card and brochures. You go to the printing websites and create attractive materials with your new business name and logo. You figure, oh, I might need 500 of these. Then, when you're ready to check out, a window pops up that reads, "Buy 500 more for only $5.99 plus tax". You figure, "I might as well go ahead, it's only a few dollars more." Then your home office is piled high with 1,000 business cards, brochures, and flyers. Not only do you have no idea where to stock this stuff, but a month down the road, you could need to change your phone number or email address. Or six months down the road your location could change. Now you're stuck with 899 promotional materials that are useless.

One year I decided to do cardboard lawn signs with my $99 promotional special. After all, I had seen tons of businesses place these signs along busy roads advertising lawn services, gold buyers, and tutoring services. I figured I'd join the lawn party. I ordered 100 signs with the sign stakes. They weren't cheap. Then I started putting up these expensive lawn signs and realized a few things I didn't know in advance. The first thing was, people steal signs and take them down. Secondly, the city, where my studio was located, didn't allow lawn signs. It was illegal. I only knew this when I got a call from city hall telling me they had my signs. Thirdly, after about two months I realized that my $99 special was too low for my studio and I was losing money. Then a year later, I closed the studio and still had about 50-60 expensive signs sitting in my basement. Even though I would have paid more per sign, I could have started with twenty signs and tested the marketing strategy before going all out.

Equipment

Buy less equipment and add on as needed. Even if you don't have a studio space, you'll need to buy a few yoga mats, blocks, blankets, straps, and bolsters. Since you'll be teaching in various places, you'll need to have those things ready to transport. With your studio space, you don't know how many students will start out. It's safe to begin with 10-15 yoga mats and an equivalent amount of yoga props. Because mats are used so frequently, don't buy high-end mats. Find a great deal at a wholesale company and buy the low-end mats. If you do this, when the mat wears out, you won't feel guilty throwing it out and replacing it with a new one. Ideally, you won't pay more than $8 per mat.

Don't buy equipment you're not sure to use. For example, I bought eye pillows thinking I was going to use them with my clients and found it was overkill. I was already covering them with blankets, and it just took too much time at the end of class. Then I was stuck with fifteen eye pillows I never used.

Space rental

I'm only referring to space rental by the hour or by the day. Be careful not to bleed out your resources to get space when you don't have registered students to fill the class. I know it's a catch 22. You need the space to advertise to get students, but you don't want to prepay and have no students. I'll teach you how you can get around it. Instead of paying an hourly fee, you can negotiate a percentage.

The first year I rented hourly space at a dance studio and signed a contract to rent at least three hours per week at $25 per hour. That was really expensive back then. A lot of times I only had one or two students, so I was losing money. Then I got smart. When I found the studio space, I ultimately rented full time, I negotiated a 30% share. So if I only got $72 in revenue for the class, I paid $21.60 for the hour. But if I made $100, she got $30. I already mentioned that I paid 10% for the church space I rented. Most studios, who rent by the hour, will want a 50% share or rent at a fixed rate. Everything in business is negotiable. Don't forget that. If a dance studio or other fitness place has certain hours with no classes, they would rather see the space filled to earn some money. Also, negotiate terms in your favor if the class doesn't pan out. Ask the place if they can apply your deposit to a new day and time and give you a couple of weeks to advertise your classes.

Get creative and grow as your income and clientele grow.

Recap of Lessons Learned: Your Business Model

1. Think about and write down what business practices are near and dear to your heart. Include principles that are musts for you and your business partner.

2. Start working on your business plan, if you're opening a studio and have a business partner, or if you're seeking financing.

3. Make a list of tasks you can delegate to others and the names of people who can help you.

4. List the top three services or products you'll provide in your yoga business.

5. Make it a habit to list the top two outcomes, for each day in your business. Have those as the main focus for your entire day.

CHAPTER SEVEN

Financial Intelligence

READ THIS CHAPTER CAREFULLY and follow the advice. I can offer you the most insight with this topic, because it's where I fell the hardest. And I'm still, in 2017, paying the price for my mistakes. I was not only careless, but also overly optimistic about my finances and financial projections. I'm going to give you the entire scoop about finances, the good, the bad, and the ugly. I want you to be fully prepared for the road ahead so you can protect your business and your family.

Start Up Funds

Some yoga businesses, and more particularly, yoga studios get financial investors, but most don't. Yoga studios are high risk with little guarantee of big returns. If you're running a yoga studio with the pressure to pay back investors, you might not stay true to your calling. That being said, you'll need startup capital. To begin your yoga business, without a partner and studio space, you'll need about $5,000 for the first year, after you pay for your yoga teacher training. Let's take a look at the costs involved to start your business, keeping in mind the money saving strategies in this book.

- Website: URL, hosting, template, images, widgets, basic design services $850
- Logo and branding $150
- Incorporation fees and business licenses $150
- Class booking software for the year $240
- Yoga equipment $300
- Promotional materials: business cards, brochures, flyers $150
- Office supplies $200
- Yoga teacher insurance per year $360
- Advertising costs for the year: Buffer, Constant Contact, Google Ad Words, Facebook ads $1,200
- Cash savings for other expenses throughout the year $1,400

If you're renting a studio space, you'll need the first month's rent and a security deposit. You'll also need to place a security deposit with the electric company and possibly for your Internet and phone as well. You'll have the additional expenses of furnishing your studio and in some cases you'll have the expense of interior remodeling if the space doesn't fit your needs.

There are many ways you can get start up capital, but all of them are not created equal. Here are some ways you can procure your start up capital with the pros and cons.

1. You can loan your company the start up funds.
The advantage of this is that you can pay yourself back over the course of several years. Put a cap on the amount you lend to your company and stick to it. Integrate the pay back plan, for your startup loan, into your business plan.

2. You can borrow the money from family members.
Be careful with this one. When I signed a three-year lease for my studio space, I asked my dad to lend me $25,000 to pay off debt so I could get a business loan. *I know, right? Crazy logic, a loan to get a loan? Look don't judge. But don't do it.* I needed it at the time, but I regret having done it. Borrowing money from a bank is one thing, but putting a relationship on the line is a whole other ballgame. When you form a company, whether it's an LLC or an S Corporation, you're protected if your company goes belly up. The creditors can't come after your personal assets. However, if your company goes bankrupt or closes due to financial reasons, as mine did, you will still owe the money back to your family or friends. To this day, I'm still paying my dad back for the money he loaned me. And I still owe him a lot of money.

Please learn from my setback, relationships come first, money comes second. Try not to borrow money from family and if you do, pay them back first, before your credit cards and business loans.

3. You can use a business credit card.

With your Employer Identification Number (EIN), you can take out a credit card under your business name. Credit card companies are pretty generous with lines of credit for businesses. But again, proceed with caution. When a credit card company gives you a credit line of $10,000, it can be easy to charge it up. While a business card is a better option to borrowing money from a family member, remember you're paying interest. Even if they give you 12-months interest-free, it's not likely that you'll be able to pay off the $5,000 in start up money within the first year.

4. Business loans.

Banks have gotten more conservative after the housing crisis of 2008. It's much more difficult to get a business loan today. I got a small business loan after I had been in business four years. You have to show a detailed business plan, bank statements from your business accounts, balance sheets, income, business tax returns, a marketing plan, and give them your first-born child. Okay, I'm kidding about the first-born child, but it was a big deal. I only borrowed $12,000, which is small by business standards, but I had to show a lot of proof that the business could be successful. *And we all know how that went down.*

Once you register your company, you will get loads of solicitations for business loans. Do not call when you receive those letters. They will give you money, but at an interest rate of 20-30% or more. Never pay more than 10% on a business loan.

Whichever way you decide to get your startup capital, take into account that you will need to be frugal in the first few years. Shop Craigslist, Ebay, or yard sales when you can to get business equipment like printers, or chairs for your waiting room. Stay under your $5,000, not including studio rent and you'll start making a profit sooner.

Budget

Make a budget for your yoga business and stick to it. Separate your personal finances from your business finances. Some things will overlap, but make a decision now where you will put them. For example, if you plan on using your cell phone for your business, put cell phone expenses in your yoga business budget.

I'm going to assume you've never done a business budget. So the first thing I'm going to do is to direct you to budgeting software. If you're savvy with Microsoft Excel or Apple Numbers, you can do a budget on a simple spreadsheet. You can also buy software such as Quicken, which I've heard has gone downhill. Two other top-rated budgeting software services are YNAB (You Need a Budget), which is free for 34-days and $4.17 per month afterward (https://www.youneedabudget.com/) and Budget Pulse, which is free (https://www.budgetpulse.com/).

Here are some of the categories you want to include in your yoga business budget:

- Teacher pay, including yourself
- Taxes: local, state, sales tax, employment tax etc.
- Studio rent or space rent
- Utilities (Electricity, water, gas)
- Internet and office phone
- Cell phone
- Website expenses
- Merchant processing fees
- Office supplies
- Equipment
- Advertising
- Travel fees (gasoline, toll, car maintenance)
- Food/ Entertainment
- Interest charges and bank fees
- Yoga clothing (for yourself)
- Insurance
- Business association fees (Yoga Alliance), business licenses, corporation fees

Once you set up your budget and know your expenses, you can set up your income for cash flow.

Cash Flow

It's important to know how much is going out each month to know what has to come in. Another big mistake I made was not paying myself right away. In your budgeting, include how much you need in income per month and if you have your business partner, include his or her income too. Even if you pay yourself a small salary in the first year, pay yourself a salary. You have personal bills and expenses and you can't starve yourself or rack up debt on credit cards to make ends meet.

Once you do this, you'll know how much revenue your yoga business needs to make each month. Although you've accounted for many of your monthly expenses in advance, with your startup funds, you need to plan as if those expenses are not paid for. Let's suppose, with all of your business expenses and your personal salary you need $6,000 per month in revenue. Take that figure up to $7,000 per month and stick to it. You will need to accumulate at least three months in savings and ideally six months to cover slow months. Put the extra $1,000 per month in a separate business savings account and don't touch it.

The fitness business has high and low seasons. Throughout the year it tends to average out. But you will have at least three slow months, in a year, and you need to have money in savings to plan for those months. I've been in business close to nine years and I've noticed that while January is a booming month, February is always a down month. Another typical slow month is August. There are always exceptional years, but you'll go into a panic if you don't plan for these slow months.

Once you figure out your absolute must in revenue, you can backtrack and calculate how many classes you must teach and how much revenue per class you must make. With gross revenue of $7,000 per month, you will need to teach on average 12 classes weekly and make $150 per class. Do you see how this works?

You will also need capital to run your business on a day-to-day basis. Sometimes expenses come up that you can't foresee. For example, a toilet might overflow, a computer breaks down, or your cell phone cracks. You will have about $1,400 of your startup capital to cover these unforeseen expenses. Taking the target revenue from the example above, if you make more than $7,000 in revenue for the month, put the rest in the account for running capital. Keep a buffer of at least $1,500 to $2,000 in your business checking account at all times.

Crazy unforeseen story from my studio

One spring I was teaching a three-day Ayurvedic and yoga retreat at my studio. I had six lovely ladies attend and things were going fabulously all weekend. I had hired my 17-year-old son to help out and all was well. The third day, when we were going through an emotional healing exercise, a very intense experience, one of my students went to the bathroom and flushed the toilet, which started to overflow like crazy. Water and other items were running everywhere. I asked my son to run in and turn off the water switch at the bottom of the toilet. The toilet back up couldn't have come at a worse time. But it was rather hilarious timing too. I was having my students write letters to people they needed to forgive. Then, to let go of the emotional baggage, I was going to have them throw rocks into the stream, out behind the studio, to release any negative energy. It was going to be a powerful and magical exercise.

Well, the toilet situation was a more immediate call. Since my son didn't have his driver's license, I had to go buy supplies to unclog the toilet and clean up the bathroom. A little disappointed, I sent my students outside to do the activity by themselves. Then, I drove quickly over to Kmart to buy a plunger, gloves, disinfectant wipes, a mop, and a bucket. I didn't have any of these things because my studio came with a daily cleaning service. Twenty minutes later, I was back in the studio plunging the toilet. Luckily, everyone was good-natured about the whole situation. They even joked that the exercise was so powerful, that the toilet felt it needed to release too.

Tax Deductible Items

One of the best financial perks of running your own business is that you get to deduct expenses from your taxes. You can deduct pretty much anything that pertains to your business. And when you're self-employed or a business owner of an LLC or C or S Corporation, most things fall under a business expense.

The reality of life as a business owner is that there is often very little separation between you and your business. For example, I work from home most of time. But when I go out to sit at a coffee place or eat lunch at a restaurant, I'm usually doing business in one form or another. I'm, either checking my emails, taking calls, texting clients, or writing my books. The money I spend at those establishments, while I'm working, is tax deductible. When I travel to take my kid to college or for a conference or event, my work comes with me. All of my travel expenses are tax deductible. Even when I'm on vacation, I'm usually spending two to three hours daily working. And so guess what? My vacations are tax deductible.

You can also tax deduct your home office or if you have a studio in your home, you can deduct that as well. Since I have a home office and home studio, I take the square footage of both in relation to the square footage in my home and deduct the percentage used for business. You can equally deduct a percentage of your utilities to cover your home office space. Business tax software or an accountant will guide you through calculating the deduction for your home office.

Lastly, if you're driving your car for your business, you can deduct the gas, mileage, maintenance, and interest on car payments. You'll need to keep track of how many miles you're driving daily for work and what percentage of time you're using the car for work versus personal use.

If you're working as a sole proprietor, an LLC, or an S Corporation, you will likely do your taxes once per year. If your yoga studio is going gangbusters, which I hope it does, and bringing in more than $10,000 per month, you may have to file business taxes quarterly. Please consult with a tax accountant if that's the case. That being said, if you're filing once a year, you need to have an organization system to keep track of your tax-deductible items. Here are a few tips to make tax day easier.

1. Keep all of your receipts.
You must always ask for paper receipts for tax deductions. Keep all of your receipts in a central location, in an envelope marked with the year. January first, I always bring out another big envelope and mark "Business Taxes" then add the year. I stuff all of my receipts in that en-

velope throughout the year. If the IRS audits you, you'll need those receipts.

2. Have one credit card and one debit card for all business spending.

It's a nightmare to arrive at the beginning of a new year, as you're preparing to file your business taxes, and realize you can't track all of your expenses because you have no idea which cards you used. You need to track and identify the exact amounts and match the receipts to the proper account. Having one major credit card and one business checking account, with a linked debit card, will make accounting a lot easier.

3. Track your deductible business expenses on a software program like Quickbooks.

Unless you're an accountant, learn how to use simple accounting software or have someone teach you. You can also create categories on a Microsoft Excel or Apple Numbers spreadsheet and enter the numbers each month. Over the years, I've kept good records, but I've waited until I do my business taxes to complete this crucial step. Tax week, as I call it, is painful and tedious. Create time and track your deductible expenses once a month.

> Wow! This is heavy so far. Get up and do an upward dog, because you're going up baby! Then, do tree pose because you're growing and so is your business. No, seriously, get up now. Do it. Shake it out. Take a few deep breaths because it's tax time.

Filing Taxes

Tax time shouldn't be scary. It's not Halloween after all; it's the New Year and time to celebrate!

I was shaking in my winter boots, the first time I had to file business taxes. I was so nervous that I hired the tax accountant at my credit union. Since my taxes were so simple, according to the accountant, he actually forgot me among the pile of tax returns. Not knowing what was happening, I was chewing on my nails, in anticipation, thinking I did something wrong and the IRS was out to get me. When April 15th was approaching, I called the accountant inquiring about my taxes. After all, I didn't want them to be late. He apologetically told me that he had forgotten about me and informed me that my taxes were already late since business taxes must be filed by March 15th. So he filed an extension and gave me my tax forms a couple of weeks later. In the end, he gave me a four-page document. *I expected it to be like twenty. Because, hello? Those were business taxes.* I looked at it, looked at him, shook my head, and signed it. I lost money the first year, so there wasn't any big deal to the tax forms. After dealing with this tax clown, who took four months to do four pages, I decided to do my taxes on my own. And it's been fine.

I'm not suggesting you do your business taxes on your own, I'm suggesting that you can. In past years I've used Turbo Tax. Since I have an Apple computer, Intuit, who owns Turbo Tax, has not come out with software for C and S Corporations that are Mac friendly. I had to borrow other people's computers to do my business taxes. Plus, I've found that Turbo Tax prices have gone up and their accuracy has gone down. A couple of years ago, I found Tax Act (https://www.taxact.com/) and fell in love. Their software is user friendly and inexpensive. You can do your business taxes on their site, so you don't have to download software. They ask the right questions and because they do, your taxes will be accurate. Doing and filing taxes with Tax Act will cost you about 50% less than Turbo Tax.

Dates you need to respect

If you have contractors working for you, you need to file 1099s with the IRS before January 31st. Contractors are people, who you pay for part-time services, but for whom you don't withhold taxes. In other words, they're not employees. A contractor could be a yoga teacher or other fitness teacher, an admin, or anyone else you've paid to do work for you. When they start, have them fill out a W-9 form. Then, if over the course of the year, you pay them more than $600 total, you must fill out a 1099-MISC and give two copies to the contractor, one for state and one for federal, and send one copy to the IRS. You must postmark them before January 31st. You can file these online with many companies and pay between $3.00 and $6.00 per 1099 filing.

As I mentioned in my accountant snafu above, you will need to file your federal business taxes before March 15th. Check your state for business state tax due dates.

Also, if you're selling items for retail sale, you'll have to collect and pay sales tax to your state. Register with your state's taxation website and elect to pay sales taxes once per month or once per quarter. Don't ignore this or you will pay hefty late fees and penalties.

Know what's going on in your finances

Whether you have an accountant or not, it's important to know exactly what's going on in your finances. Ultimately, you are responsible for your company's financial health. Get informed and don't rely on your accountant or business partner to be in the know. You can get hit pretty hard if you discover one day that your finances aren't at the level you had imagined.

Recap of Lessons Learned: Finances

1. Get $5,000 for your startup capital, not including studio rent or utilities.

2. Make a budget for your business and separate your personal finances from your business.

3. Save at least $1,000 monthly for slow months until you have three-six months of expenses saved up.

4. Keep between $1,500 and $2,000 in your business checking account for running expenses.

5. Create a system for tracking and logging your business expenses.

6. Decide whether or not you will hire an accountant to do your business taxes or tackle them yourself.

7. Keep an eye on the due dates for all tax related filings.

8. Even if you hand off your finances to a business partner or third party, keep watch of what's going on at least twice per month.

CHAPTER EIGHT

Opening & Running a Successful Yoga Studio

MAKING THE DECISION TO open your own yoga studio can be exciting, exhilarating, and scary at the same time. Your mind is churning with creative ideas on what you want your studio to look like, how you'll interact with clients, and how you'll be making a great living by doing what you love. But you also want to minimize wrong moves. If you did the modeling exercise in chapter six, you're already better prepared than most people who want to open a yoga studio. If you haven't done it yet, go through the exercise before you start looking for a studio space. Selecting the right business partner, studio location, hiring the right employees, and planning for a successful launch will all be crucial to the success of your studio. Make sure to follow the advice step by step and don't take short cuts. Finally, have fun and enjoy the process. This is a unique opportunity and special time in your life.

Step One: Choose Your Business Partner

Selecting a business partner is a bit like selecting a mate. Scrutiny is required and assessment of personality traits and value system are essential. If you're thinking of opening a yoga studio by yourself, I would advise you to rethink your strategy. I believe my number one downfall was trying to do everything alone. Think about it. When you have a business partner, you can take vacations, take days off, and have a life from time to time. Even if you're gone, there is someone else running the studio and the business is still generating income. When you need to make major business decisions, you have another invested person who can bring ideas to the table and set you straight when you get off course.

Many entrepreneurs are control freaks. *Don't get on the defensive! You know this to be true.* This is your baby. You've nurtured this dream. However, you're going to have to let go of control if you want your business to flourish. And I know you do.

I acknowledge that this is your idea, your dream, and your studio. I'm assuming that you're the providing the startup capital for your company. If you're already going into your yoga business with a designated partner and are equally investing the startup capital, you can skip over this section. However, if you're about to launch your business and need a superstar to come on board as your partner, read on.

I learned this business partner strategy through leader and business genius, Tony Robbins, at his live event, Unleash the Power Within. Take the following steps to select your business partner.

1. Business Rock Star

Find a yoga teacher who is a superstar in the business. You want a person who already attracts a lot of clients, whom people love, and who has a great resume in the yoga world. When you have your prospective business partner, have him or her take the DISC personality profile https://www.tonyrobbins.com/disc/, after you take it first. You want a person who compliments your strengths, not someone who has the same strengths as you. For example, if you're more of an introvert, you want a partner who is an extravert. If you are a big risk-taker, you want a partner who's a little more conservative.

As you select the right person, use your head, but also use your intuition. Does it feel like the one you're choosing is a person of integrity? Is he or she out to make money or is this person invested in your vision? Do his or her references check out? Is he or she willing to put in the hours necessary to make the business flourish? Does he or she have a passion for yoga teaching and living yoga off the mat? Is he or she a person of action? The answers to these questions are important. You might have a person experienced in yoga, but who is not a leader or who doesn't have enough time to invest.

In the first couple of years, you will both be working a lot. Running a business is no joke. You don't want a business partner who loves teaching, but who doesn't love all of the other things that come with running a business. You also don't want a person who has a lot of creative ideas, but who isn't good at taking action. You need balance.

2. Business split

When you find your partner, write up a contract to give them 49% equity in your company. You get 51% because you founded your company and you provided the startup capital. Your name is the only name on the business bank accounts. You sign the checks.

3. Money split

With your monthly revenue, after expenses are paid, you take off the first 25%. You pocket the first 10% to start paying yourself back, for the invested startup funds, and because it's your company. Then, the next 15% goes toward training and future education to take your business to the next level. Split the remaining 75% between you and your business partner.

I'm not a lawyer, nor do I play one on TV. Consult a lawyer, versed in business contracts, to draw up the agreement between you and your business partner. This agreement will also be a part of your Articles of Incorporation and integrated into your business plan. Do not simply make a "Gentleman's Agreement". You need to have everything written down, signed by both parties, and notarized.

Step Two: Choosing Your Studio Space

In business, location is everything. Renting a business property can be costly and you don't want to overreach. Yes, it would be ideal to rent a space in a fancy shopping plaza, but rarely do yoga studios make enough money to support the fancy rent. I shared with you the story of my friend who rented a space in a high-end shopping center near a high traffic grocery store. I also shared with you that her studio went belly up within 18 months. It doesn't matter if you hold classes 24/7, there is no justification for high rent. You and your business partner need to make a living. And how do you expect to be in a Zen state teaching about peace, serenity, and present-moment awareness if you're both freaking out about the upcoming rental payment?

That being said, you need a location that's easy to find, has ample parking space, and is in a high traffic area. You also want to find a space that has well-insulated walls or is far away from noisy businesses. Choose a space that has at least one restroom, per 15 clients, inside of your space. Many office buildings have common restrooms in the hallway. This is completely impractical for a yoga studio, since a lot of clients will come from work and need to change. You don't necessarily need a changing room, but have a space where clients can hang coats, bags, and cubby space to put purses and other personal items. I bought a shelving unit at Costco that had canvas square baskets and it worked perfectly.

In addition, try to find a space on the main floor. If you're holding classes for students of varied ages, you need to think about people with limited mobility coming in for yoga therapy or moms coming in with babies for Mom & Baby yoga. If you select a space on the 2nd or 3rd floor, make sure there's an elevator. My studio was on the main floor. But you wouldn't believe how many calls I would get in a month asking me if there were stairs to climb to get to the studio.

> This is the fun part! I know you're as excited as I was. Let's go shopping for a yoga studio space!

"I need a bigger space!"

When you're looking at empty business spaces, it can be difficult to imagine how many students you can fit in the space. Let me give you a frame of reference. My studio, including two offices and a bathroom, was 900 square feet. Myself included, the studio space fit about fifteen yoga students comfortably in the class. Use that as a frame of reference for how many students you'd like to have in your classes. If you want 30 students in a class, double that amount to 1,800 square feet. In the beginning, try not to rent a studio that holds more than thirty in a class. Already, it's challenging to fill a class of thirty, unless you're running a Bikram yoga studio, where I've heard they fit fifty. Plus, you can always grow into a bigger space as time goes on.

"But it's butt ugly!"

As you're touring spaces, don't look at esthetics. Part of your leasing contract will include redecorating. When I signed my business lease, I told them I wanted new carpeting and fresh paint. I got to choose the colors for both and it was all included. They also included a sign for the outside and signs for the door of the studio. If the property management needs to move walls or install a new bathroom, the cost will be rolled into your rental payments.

"Thirty dollars per square foot, WTF?"

When I began searching for yoga studio space, I had no idea how business leasing worked. So when I saw an ad that said, "$30 per square foot" for a 1,000-square foot space, I panicked. There was no way on God's green earth I could pay $30,000 per month. Well, in fact, business rentals work by the year, not by the month. In this example, your rent would be $2,500 per month, which is much better. However, $30 per square foot is not a good deal so let's talk about how you can do better.

"I like the space, but…"

Once you've found a couple of spaces you like and both you and your business partner agree upon, it's time to negotiate. Everything in business is negotiable. If you're not used to negotiating, get used to it. In business contracts there are not only additional fees, for renovation or building improvement, but also, most business rental agreements write in a rental raise, by a percentage, for each year of the contract. So you want to start your contract as low as possible. If they're offering the space at

$30 per square foot, ask for $23 per square foot. If they say $24, take it. If they say $25, offer $24. If they say no, walk away, temporarily. Tell them you want to look at other more affordable spaces. Go to the other space you like and do the same thing. If there is one that you prefer, make a list of all the updates that must be done to the space and present it to the property manager. If they can include all of the updates for $25 per square foot and agree to it, take it. Do you see how this works?

You can negotiate better if you sign a longer contract too. My hardcore advice to you is to only sign a three-year lease or less. Business leases are extremely hard to get out of and you don't want to be stuck if your business doesn't take off.

In this order, here is what you need to negotiate:

1. Cost per square foot

2. Renovations and updates: paint, carpet, signs, moving walls, removing doors, updating bathrooms

3. The fees for building maintenance, usually assessed once or twice per year

4. The percentage increase each year

5. Ask to include housekeeping services in the contract.

6. The length of your lease

"Can I sign now?"

Before you sign, ask them about rules for subleasing. You absolutely want an out if you can't fulfill your contract. Or if you find the studio has a slow period or you or your partner gets sick and you need to sublease part of the space, you need to know the rules.

Ask them how much insurance you need to carry. Each city or county has its own requirements for insurance. There are specific insurances for yoga studios. An individual yoga teacher insurance policy will not suffice for a studio space. You will need insurance to cover your studio and all of the teachers who teach under your roof. *Or on top of it, depending on where you hold your classes.* For my studio, I used Philadelphia Insurance Company. They have insurance specific to Fitness and Wellness (https://www.phly.com/productsfw/default.aspx).

Next, read through your lease line by line. If you have questions about any words or clauses, ask before you sign. Understand exactly what's covered and what's not. For example, I wasn't aware that light bulb replacement was covered under my lease until about six months into it. But a service like that could easily save you $100 per year. In business, everything adds up.

Breathe! Now, you're ready to sign.

Step Three: Hiring

In the beginning, as you're opening your studio, hire as few people as possible to keep your overhead low. You might need a person to handle the phones, be at the front desk, and conduct sales. And you might need a teacher or two or maybe not. It will take a few months to get off the ground and fill your classes. So think about how many classes you will be offering weekly. Let's start with a number. Suppose you need to run about four classes daily or about twenty-eight classes per week. You and your business partner can teach about ten classes each to begin, so that's twenty. Keep in mind that some of these classes might not even have one student in the first month. That leaves eight classes left. It's possible to find one teacher to cover four classes, for the first three months, and have the remaining four off the schedule until your client base grows. And there you have it.

Finding your peeps

You've got your business started. You have your studio space. Now you need to hire some people. It can be a little nerve wrecking in the beginning. This is your baby and your bread and butter. You want to make sure the people you hire will stay true to your vision. Intuition will be really important in this category, but also do your homework. Check out everything about the person you intend to hire. Call references. Do a simple background check. Look at the candidate's social media accounts. First do a phone interview, then an in person interview, and audition for a yoga teacher. Have them take a personality profile test.

To find people, I ran a paid ad on Craigslist. For $25 you can run a help wanted ad for one month. You can also ask around at yoga teacher training programs or your yoga studio.

Hiring your admin

For a yoga studio, you won't need a full-time employee for the front desk. At most, you'll need one to answer phones and greet customers in the evenings and on Saturday mornings when you're the busiest. Your front desk admin should also have sales experience. The best person to hire will be a motivated high school student with a car or a college student who's attending school locally. They won't mind being paid minimum wage, or a little more and they will be happy for the experience. As a perk, offer them free yoga classes if they work more than 10 hours per week.

When hiring your admin, don't just go on personality during the interview. Check the resume for details. Look at references and call them. When I hired my summer interns, I asked for GPAs. I only hired interns with a GPA of 3.5 or greater. I wanted students who were in honors societies, clubs, and activities. You want one or two outgoing young adults, who aren't afraid to talk to people and who have a great work ethic. Ask for teacher recommendations.

One other thing I learned from Tony Robbins about hiring is, only hire people with great, sunny smiles and happy eyes. If you look into their eyes and you see sadness or anger, do not hire them.

Once you hire your admin, train them the way you want them trained. Their attitude and sales pitch must match your company philosophy.

Hiring yoga teachers

When you hire your first teacher, you might not have time to go through the following process. But for subsequent teachers, I would suggest you try this. It worked for me. And it also helped weed out potential teachers who were not serious and committed.

Almost every teacher I hired at my studio had to do a six-week unpaid internship with me. I took newly trained yoga teachers or even seasoned yoga teachers. They had to take two of my classes every week and I would train them before and after class to the specifications of the studio. During the course of the internship, they would slowly take over parts of the class, teaching one or two sections at a time until they had taught every part of the class. During the internship, they could attend any class in the studio for free.

The internship gave the intern time to learn about the studio and my expectations. It gave them the time to get to know the regular clients. I got to see the intern's work ethic, such as whether or not they arrive on time, are clean and professional looking, and how they interact with people. I got to know them personally to see if we could develop mutual trust. The internship step was extremely important to my business. Here's why. When you hire yoga teachers to teach classes at your studio, you're rarely in the studio. They come in to teach when you have time off. Generally, you're not inside the yoga room when they are teaching. So you need to be 100% certain that they embody the philosophy of the studio. You want your teachers to follow the studio's commitment to excellent customer service, and to be outstanding people in general. You can only be certain, if you spend a significant amount of time seeing them in action.

A handful of teachers in the internship program didn't make it through. Some of them were not committed to an excellent work ethic and dropped out when they saw my rigorous standards. I only had to ask a couple to leave.

My advice to you is to have rigorous standards for your teachers. Create guidelines for them to follow. People need structure. For example, I had a "no class outline" rule, which meant that teachers could not have a lesson plan or index cards on their mat in front of the class. It looks incredibly unprofessional. Yet, I taught my teachers how to have a clean class structure, so they wouldn't need an outline. Other rules you might consider, for your yoga teachers, are things like no advertising other classes or workshops at other studios, or no gossiping about other teachers or employees. Everything you will not tolerate, you need to have written out. Then have all new hires sign them.

Another revelation I found out, by trial and error, was to never give more than four classes to a single hired teacher. You'll find that most yoga teachers have full time jobs. Others, who are not working full time, might have children at home. I discovered that yoga teachers, in those categories, are overly optimistic about what they can handle. At the interview they assure you they can teach 3-4 classes per week. As God is my witness, every single one of the yoga teachers I hired, over the course of seven years, who said they could and would teach three to four classes weekly, scaled back within the first month. The only exception to this rule, are yoga teachers whose full-time job is being a yoga teacher and who do not have kids or who are empty nesters. Follow this hiring guideline to save you a *lot* of pain and headaches.

- Give yoga teachers, who have a full time job or who have kids under eighteen at home, at most two classes weekly on the schedule. If they want to teach more, they go on the sub list.

- Give yoga teachers, who are either full-time yoga teachers, retired, or empty nesters, at most four yoga classes weekly on the schedule.
- Have a sub list. All teachers on staff can sub for each other. In addition, have one or two subs you can use for emergencies.

Lastly, all yoga teachers are independent contractors. Pay your yoga teachers per class and don't pay more than a competitive rate. In your market study, get the teacher pay rates of the ten studios you visited in your area. For example, if the average pay is $30 per class, you can offer to pay $32.50 per class. Two friends, who recently opened yoga studios, told me that the number one demise of new yoga studios is overpaying their teachers. I was in that category, my friend. I wanted to be generous and kind and I wanted loyal teachers. That's fine, but you have to meet your bottom line first.

Step Four: Plan Your Business Launch

This is the moment you've been waiting for. You've been in the planning stages for months and now it's finally happening. You feel giddy and also a bit nervous. What if no one shows up? What if people don't like our location? *What if they hate my dress? Oops, wrong event. You know what I mean.*

It's easy to get carried away with the details. But the most important part of a launch is to get people to your studio. A great way to insure that you'll have paying customers coming through your door on opening day, is to do a coupon offer with Groupon, Living Social, or another company in your area. Have the deal offered two to three weeks before your opening day. You can also plan a big party, sell tickets, and do a raffle for a free month of yoga. You could have demonstrations, healthy food, tea, a local author, a tarot reader, musicians, or anything that will attract people to your studio. Put the studio launch in the local newspaper under weekend events. Post flyers around town. Create a Facebook event for your business page. Or you could have a fundraiser on the same day at your studio. For example, talk to the coach of a cheerleading squad, at the local high school, and offer the parking lot space at your studio for a car wash. Then have the cheerleaders raise money by washing cars. It will attract people. Include a children's event at your studio, even if you aren't holding kids classes right away. It will attract the parents.

Get with your business partner and brainstorm creative ways to make your studio launch a huge success.

Step Five: Plan for Growth

Believe it or not, your little baby studio will grow up one day. You will have nurtured and cared for it. As your business grows, think of ways you can make it more profitable so that you and your partner can increase your salaries, save for the future, open a bigger studio, and eventually sell your business one day.

Maximizing your studio space

Even if you have five classes per day in the studio, there will still be a large portion of the day where the space isn't being used. You're still paying rent for that time. So why not fill the space and earn money toward rent in the process? You can decide what business people would be a good fit and then advertise. For example, you could rent to a massage therapist, a Tai Chi teacher, an early morning boot camp instructor, or a daytime knitting group. The possibilities are endless and you can rent by the hour or half day. Try to find people who will be consistent and who can sign a monthly contract. For example, let's say Bob, the Tai Chi teacher, wants to rent the space on Tuesday and Thursday mornings from 6-8 a.m. every week. You could charge him $25 per hour or $400 per month. Or if he signs a monthly contract for three months, you could give him a break and charge $350 per month. You will be guaranteed that amount for at least three months and Bob has a space. If you think creatively, you could have other businesses pay for most of your rent.

Other services and products

As time goes on, you will want to offer your customers other services and perhaps, products. Many yoga studios offer yoga teacher trainings and feel it's a good way to not only generate income, but to train teachers who might eventually teach at the studio. Once your studio is well established, you don't need to stop there. I know a studio, with a separate office space, that has a massage therapist come in two days per week. Other studios offer Ayurvedic consultations or nutritional consultations.

I know studio owners who organize kids birthday parties on the weekends at the studio. I did bridal bachelorette parties for brides who wanted to take the girls to yoga before going out for the night.

As I mentioned, products are nice to have and offer, but it's difficult to make a whole lot of money selling products. However, food items are a great way to generate extra income. If you don't have a beverage and food license, you can still sell prepackaged food at your front desk. Go to a wholesale store like Costco and buy big cases of water, Vitamin water, power bars, etc. and sell them individually. You can mark up food items considerably, because you're offering them for convenience. Buy a used commercial fridge, with a clear glass door, and stock it up with waters, juices, cold teas. Have your front desk person take care of sales transactions.

Recap of Lessons Learned: Opening a Studio

1. Start talking to people in your local yoga community and see who might be the right fit to become your business partner. If you already have a business partner, start talking about dividing the tasks before you open.

2. When selecting your studio space, take into consideration parking, location, foot traffic, other business traffic, the amount per square foot, and the ability to modify the space if needed.

3. Negotiate everything in business, especially your rental space.

4. Hire with your intuition, but also with heavy scrutiny. You don't want any surprises once you've handed your studio over to someone else for the night.

5. Brainstorm creative ideas for your business launch. Make it a smashing success!

6. Have a list of business growth ideas to try every few months. Never stagnate. Always have something in the pipeline.

CHAPTER NINE

Balancing Work & The Rest of Your Life

IF YOU'RE A WOMAN, who has ever had a baby, you know the feeling of not knowing where the baby ends and where you begin. For months during pregnancy, your bodies are literally molded into one. Then when you give birth, your baby is attached to some part of your body, for what seems like two years. At some point during that second year, you feel like, "Ugh, when am I finally going to feel like myself again?"

Opening and running a business is no different. For a long time, you and your business are one. You won't see the delineation. Every line in your life is fuzzy. Every thought, feeling, and action seems to move around your growing business. And every person in your life, who is not a business owner, can't understand this.

Owning a business is not for the weak at heart or feeble minded. Pardon my French, but you're a badass for wanting to run a business in the first place. Yet, as hard as you're going to work and as motivated as you are, you'll need to find balance in your life.

You Can't Give Away What You Don't Have

Both the problem and the beauty of being a yoga teacher is that you're a caretaker and healer. You have a deep desire to make everyone happy and healthy. You give a lot of yourself because you truly have everyone's best interest at heart. Yet, in the midst of prancing through the fields, with your basket of love, giving it away to everyone, you can forget to take care of yourself. Burnout is such a common occurrence with people who are healers.

You are so strong. I know you're strong or persistent; otherwise you wouldn't be all the way toward the end of this book. All joking aside, I know you're strong because you are seriously considering teaching yoga as a career. You could be doing a million other things and make a whole lot more money, but you're interested in serving. That makes you an amazing person.

In your strength, you need to let others take care of you. You need to learn ways you can take care of yourself daily. When you take yoga, as a student, you feel refreshed. You receive so much during your class. After yoga, you feel exhilarated and powerful. But did you ever wonder why you feel so incredible at the end of class? It's because your teacher, your guide, gave so much of him or herself during class. Now, you're that teacher. You must remember how much you're giving when you teach. You give away body, mind, emotions, and soul.

After teaching five or ten classes weekly, you can quickly become depleted of energy.

You Are Never a Guru in Your Own Home

One of my favorite gurus, Dr. Wayne W. Dyer, a famous author and speaker, used to joke that he was never a guru in his own home. He said, "You're a dork in your own home." He used to tell the story about walking his dog at night and his neighbor would joke, "How is the father of motivation walking his own dog?" He answered, "I have eight kids and don't have one called 'motivation'. I can't get any of my kids motivated enough to walk the dog."

I can attest to that. When my eldest was in sixth grade, his teacher said, "What does your mom do for a living?" He answered, "She teaches people how to levitate." Upon hearing this I went a little ballistic. I said, "You can't tell people that! They're going to think I'm crazy." My child looked up at me innocently and said, "Well, that's what you do. Don't you?" My children, all three of them, have very little knowledge of what I do. They have almost zero interest in yoga, meditation, or Ayurveda. Jay, the one who said I taught levitation, is highly skeptical of alternative medicine. My middle child, Mat, has done a little mediation with me. But the little one just knows, "Mommy is a little famous. Her books are in the library and at Barnes & Noble." Other than that, I'm just mom.

You could be a TV star and your family just knows your job takes you away from them. They see the other side of you. Don't get discouraged when they don't feel your enthusiasm about what you do. They won't really be interested in whose life you've influenced and whom you've met.

It can be difficult too when your significant other isn't on the same spiritual path. You can get frustrated when you're talking about an epiphany you had during meditation and he responds with, "Do you know what time the game starts?" Or when you're telling her, "Babe, I conquered this hard pose in yoga today." And she responds with, "Did you see my red dress?" It feels as if you're talking straight over their heads. And you are somewhat.

Be patient with the people in your life. Some will be jealous because you're living the dream. You're doing exactly what you love and getting paid. Most people hate their jobs and so they falsely believe that if you love yours, it's not a serious job. Send them love and compassion. You don't have to justify what you do. You know your job is right for you and that's all that matters.

Your family might take it poorly when they have to pick up the extra slack because you're working so much. Then, feeling guilty, you do more than you should at home. That's how burnout occurs. Practice delegating tasks to others so you have enough energy to spend time freely with your family and have leisure time for yourself.

At home, be grateful that they don't see you as the guru, but as a spouse, lover, parent, or friend. You'll need that love and support moving forward.

Michelle's Top Ten for Living a Balanced Life

For several years, I used to unconsciously punish myself by working too hard. I felt if I wasn't making enough money, I must not be working hard enough. So I'd work harder, put in longer hours, and ponder new strategies to gain more clients. I wouldn't let myself relax except when I was asleep. In a way, it's good for you, because the result of all of that overwork is this book. But eventually I learned that I needed to find a balance between work and the rest of my life. In this section I'm going to share with you my top ten must-dos for living a balanced life.

1. Meditate.

If you don't have a meditation practice, start now. Since 2007, meditation has completely transformed my life. The pressures of running a business are enormous and it can be easy to get caught up in your head. Get in the habit of mediating every day. You will be calmer, make better decisions, and be a more effective teacher and leader overall.

2. Put down the cell phone.

The constant demands of calls, texts, and emails, will wear you down. Not to mention when you're with your kids or significant other, it's not fair to them if you're completely absorbed on your phone. Set a time of day when you decide the phone is away from your body. All of the unanswered correspondence can wait until the next day. For example, if you set your time at 8 p.m., put the phone in a place you can't see it or set the phone to "do not disturb". Believe me, I've had clients who absolutely had "yoga emergencies" at 9, 10, or 11 p.m. and felt they needed to book classes at those times. It's insane. You have a life. It can wait.

3. Take at least one day off per week.

If you're not teaching yet, I know you think I'm crazy. You're thinking, "What? Of course I'll take a day off. Heck, I'll take three days off." Oh boy, you haven't met yoga world yet. When this is your full time job, you generally don't turn clients down. You get those calls for private lessons and they want Sunday night or Saturday early morning and you're inclined to agree.

I live in Northern Virginia. About a year ago, I got an inquiry to go teach a married couple private lessons in Washington D.C., about 40 minutes away. The husband wanted to surprise his wife for their anniversary and buy her a package of ten private classes. For me, that's an amazing gig. I charge $175 for a 55-minute private lesson for a couple. However, the only time they could do, in the entire week, was 8:30 p.m. on a Sunday night. That meant for the next ten weeks, I would be teaching every Sunday night until 9:30 p.m. and getting home at 10:15 p.m. But I did it. So as you can see, when opportunities arise, you take them.

Typically my day off was on Wednesdays and sometimes Sundays, but I would schedule in clients often. Now, I make sure not to schedule anything on Wednesdays and I take every other Friday off.

4. Pamper yourself.

In all honesty, I'm still working on this one. Let's make a pact to work on this together, shall we? Get a massage at least once per month. Get a manicure and pedicure every six to eight weeks. Take yoga classes to replenish your energy. Go sit in a jacuzzi or take a bath. Take care of your body and mind, you're going to need them.

5. Eat regularly.

Schedule your meals and stick to it. The nutty thing about this profession is the crazy hours you will keep. When my studio was open, I was teaching at lunchtime and dinnertime. I often got off at 9 p.m., got home at 9:30 p.m. and that's when I ate dinner. If I didn't plan my meals I was grabbing anything I could because I was so hungry. Even though I was exercising a lot, my weight started to creep up.

Bring high protein snacks to work so you don't crash and burn. In between back-to-back classes I try to eat an organic Greek yogurt or some tamari roasted almonds. If I don't do this, by the time I'm done teaching, I'm chowing down on the entire refrigerator. And God knows all of that metal and glass can't be good for you.

6. Get sleep.

Dude, why do I even have to say this? Get your beauty rest. You want to be a beautiful yogi or yogini, right? As I mentioned, your yoga business is your baby. You don't sleep a whole lot with newborns and you don't sleep a lot when you're starting a business. Before you're able to do many things on autopilot, you have to consciously think about everything. Especially if you're running a yoga studio, there are many moving parts. This is where I'm going to put on my Ayurvedic practitioner hat. According to Ayurveda, you should be in bed by 10:15 p.m. and asleep by 10:30 p.m. Wake up at 6:00 a.m. to start your day. Unless you're one of those freaks of nature, who says, "Oh, I only sleep four hours a night and I feel fantastic!" *Note the snobby, whiny voice in those quotes. You know the type. If that is you, yes, you are a freak. That is not normal! But God bless you anyway.* But for the rest of us "normal" people, we need around seven hours of sleep. Don't let your health decline because you refuse to recognize this need. You will already be running on high stress the first year and be more prone to getting colds and flus. Don't add lack of sleep to your stress.

7. Have a peer group or mastermind group.

Part of the stress of running a business is that it consumes your life, for the first few years. It seems like all you're doing is working, troubleshooting, and coming home to family demands. Your family can't be your sounding board all the time. It's not fair to them or the relationship. Form a peer group, with people outside of your studio, who are either business owners or other yoga teachers. They can be business owners with a different service, such as martial arts or dance teachers. But try to find people who run similar businesses. These are the people you can commiserate with. You can throw around ideas with these people. You can talk about what works and what doesn't.

Find people who are in a growing phase, as you are. Then, if you can, find business owners who are well established and learn from them too. Create a braintrust that will become invaluable.

8. Give your full attention to your loved ones.

Even apart from being a business owner, this is sound advice. The people who love and care for you are the most important people in your life. Our attention is so fragmented today with electronic devices. Now add in a growing business and you become even more distracted. Make a pact with yourself now that when you are spending time with your loved ones, you will give them your undivided attention. If they aren't offering you the same attention, ask them if they could. These relationships are essential for your mental wellbeing. Don't burn bridges because you're too wrapped up with work.

My boyfriend sometimes picks up his cell phone to text while we're talking. If he does that, I now stop what I'm saying and go silent. While texting, he'll look at me and say, "Continue." I'll respond, "No, I'll wait until you're done." Then I'll fall silent again. After two or three times, he gets it. That's my way of saying that it's not okay to engage in other conversations, even if they are electronic.

9. Have hobbies that don't involve yoga, meditation, or new age type stuff.

After a while, you'll become really sick of yoga. That doesn't mean you won't like it anymore. It's just going to consume a huge part of your life. In order to live a balanced life, keep up other hobbies that don't involve yoga. My hobby, that has nothing to do with yoga, is Latin dancing. When I go dance Salsa and Bachata, I don't have to think about my job at all. Even when people ask what I do, I generally avoid the topic. Dancing is an escape for me from the pressures of work.

Think about what healthy habits and activities you can have in your life to balance out the heavy physical and spiritual activities of running a yoga business.

10. Have faith.

I left this for last, because it's the most important component of all. I could not have gotten through the last nine years of my life without having strong faith. God has led me through everything and continues to lead me every day. Whatever you believe in, hold on to it with all you've got. When you're running a business you're going to need that spiritual strength. Some days, it truly is all you have. You will have pressures, bills, and, at times, nasty customers, but when you hold on to your faith, you'll stay grounded. Practice gratitude. Pray. Ask God for help. Believe that heaven has your back.

In chapter two, I talked to you about having an attitude of service to others. The best businesses are the ones who serve a higher purpose, meaning they seek to serve God first. When your focus is on serving your Higher Power, however you define it, you can't go wrong, no matter what. As you wake up each morning, start your day by saying to God, "Help me do Your will, not mine." Follow that by saying, "How can I help? And how can I serve?" If you keep God as your CEO and stay rooted in faith, you cannot make a wrong business decision.

Recap of Lessons Learned: Balancing Your Life

1.   Find ways to take care of yourself every day.

2.   Your family loves you even if they don't understand what you do.

3.   Integrate Michelle's Top Ten for a Balanced Life, little by little, until you're practicing all ten daily.

4.   Have faith that God is guiding your steps. Keep God as your CEO.

Epilogue

IN ALL OF MY trials and tribulations, it would be easy to think that even though I created a business, based on service to others, I failed. Yes, the financial failure of my business left me wondering what went wrong. But it's my faith in God, that he's directing my steps each day in every way, that led me to where I am today. To the outside world, it appears that I failed. My whole family worried about me. It hurt when my eldest said to me, "Mom, you're so poor."

It's true. In today's society, people look at success through monetary gain. Typically, if you don't make it financially, you're not successful. You need to have your vision and look at the bigger picture. Hold your financial goals. But learn to celebrate the little successes each day. The best way to do this is to have an attitude of gratitude. I've made it a daily practice to list the things I'm grateful for, in a journal, at night. What happened that brightened your day? Did a client smile at you? Did you get your first great review? Were you able to teach an inspiring class? It puts things into perspective toward the important things in life.

In my book, *The Wheel of Healing with Ayurveda*, I write about my journey with thyroid cancer. I also write about how grateful I am for that experience. There is no way I would be where I am today, and helping the number of people I do, without having gone through that illness. In the same way, I'm grateful to have run a yoga studio and failed. I learned so many lessons, many of which you've read in this book. The stamina, perseverance, hard work ethic, and character sculpted me into the person I am today. Everything you go through is preparation for the next step in your journey. Embrace it all. Love the challenges and look at them as inspiration for finding creative solutions. Keep a sense of humor at all times. Laugh at yourself when you make a mistake. Most importantly, pay it forward. Share the love and lessons you've learned with others to hold onto the true meaning of yoga; *We are all one. Namasté.*

Appendix: Ideas for Places to Teach Yoga

Here are some creative ideas to grow your yoga business.

- Create Lunch and Learn classes in corporations.
- Teach at Montessori schools and other preschools.
- Start after school programs in elementary schools.
- Have a class for teachers after school.
- Create classes in hospitals.
- Hold yoga bachelorette parties.
- Teach yoga at birthday parties.
- Create an all women or all men class.
- Go into recovery groups and offer to teach a class.
- Offer to teach in prisons or juvenlile detention centers.
- Create a Meetup group to teach intro classes.
- Plan a yoga retreat with a travel agency.
- Do a teaching vacation with an all-inclusive resort.
- Form a class at senior homes or senior living communities.
- Lead a "Yoga in the Park" class.

Books and Products

Check out Michelle's other books

The Wheel of Healing with Ayurveda: An Easy Guide to a Healthy Lifestyle (New World Library, 2015)

The Wheel of Healing with Ayurveda Companion Workbook

The Secrets of The Wheel of Healing 8-CD Set with Workbook

Help! I Think My Loved One Is an Alcoholic: A Survival Guide for Lovers, Family, & Friends

Enlightened Medicine: Your Power to Get Well Now (Fall 2017)

Chakra Healing for Vibrant Energy: Daily Practices for Balancing Your Chakras with Mindfulness, Yoga, & Meditation (New World Library, Spring 2018)

Find out more about Michelle Fondin, her books, and speaking engagements at
www.michellefondinauthor.com

Index

accountant, 7, 125-129

advertising, 4, 66, 86, 111, 117, 121, 144

asana, 15, 31, 41, 70, 89

Ayurveda, IX, 2, 19, 21, 70, 108, 109, 153, 158, 162, 165

bank accounts, 119, 135

beginner classes, 13, 59

books, 19, 21, 94, 109, 124, 126, 154, 165

brand, 12, 13, 67, 70, 71, 80-82, 117

breath, IX, 14, 25, 41, 49, 53, 126, 140

budget, 93, 120, 121, 129

Buffer, 82, 117

buffer, 123

building your business, 20, 48, 51, 55, 59, 60, 66, 80, 85, 94, 109, 136, 138, 139

business cards, 117

business credit cards, 8, 76, 98, 119, 122, 126

business model, 55, 60, 70, 97, 101, 102, 105, 107, 109, 111, 113, 118

Canfield, Jack, 54

category, 141, 145

C Corporation, 2, 5, 99-102, 107, 117, 118, 121, 124, 125, 127, 164

chakra, 20, 165

charity, 88

classes, 3-6, 8, 9, 12, 13, 16, 17,19, 25-30, 33, 37-41, 43-45, 48, 55, 56, 58, 59, 61, 66, 68, 69, 73, 76-78, 80, 82, 87-91, 103, 105, 108, 113, 122, 136, 137, 140-146, 153, 156, 157, 164

class size, X, 44

class teaching, 5, 6, 9, 12-17, 19, 20, 25-30, 32, 33, 37-44, 48, 52, 55, 60, 61, 66, 82, 87, 110, 112, 136, 143, 152, 153, 156, 157, 164

community, 9, 12, 13, 26, 31, 73, 75

competition, 43, 102

conferences, 16, 19

corporate yoga, 2, 5, 94, 99, 104, 107

customer, 7, 8, 50, 53, 55-59, 62, 68, 70, 72, 75-78, 87, 90, 91, 93, 109, 141, 143, 147, 160

ego, 27, 37, 53

emotional, 29, 52, 123

equipment, 6, 104, 112, 117, 120, 121

finances, 97, 116, 120, 129, 130

financial, 2, 33, 44-46, 65, 100, 116-119, 121, 123-125, 127, 129, 162

home, 2, 6, 8, 9, 14, 24-26, 30, 37, 44, 49, 55, 56, 63, 77, 90, 93, 97, 102, 106, 109, 111, 124, 125, 141, 144, 153-158, 164

income, 3, 6, 8, 17, 18, 26, 27, 67, 77, 90, 98, 113, 119, 121
inspiration, 7, 32, 41, 42, 81, 83, 163
insurance, 117, 121, 140
internship, 142, 143

legal, 50, 70, 97, 98, 100, 101, 104, 111
legal status, 70, 97, 98, 100, 104

marketing, 3, 8, 65-67, 69-71, 73, 75-81, 83, 85, 87-91, 93-95, 109, 111
model, 42, 55, 60, 70, 97, 99, 101-107, 109, 111, 113, 118, 132
money, X, 2, 3, 6, 8, 11, 12, 18, 19, 24, 28, 33, 44, 56-58, 61, 65, 66, 71, 72, 76, 78, 89, 91, 92, 98, 105-107, 109-111, 113, 117-120, 122, 124, 134-136, 146-148, 152, 155

negotiate, 3, 90, 113, 138, 139, 148

parents, 40, 50, 88, 146
partner, 2, 8, 70, 88, 99, 102, 105, 113, 114, 117, 121, 129, 130, 133-136, 138-140, 146, 148
paying yourself, 92, 118, 121, 135
philosophy, 15, 21, 61, 104, 105, 142, 143
poses, 41-43, 83, 97
pranayama, 14, 15
price, 12, 68, 69, 88, 107, 116, 127
products, 3, 66, 94, 108, 109, 114, 140, 147, 148, 165
professional relationship, 49, 50

referrals, 87
Registered Yoga Teacher, 15, 31
reputation, 9, 48-51, 53, 55, 57-63, 81, 82
resume, 106, 134, 142
retreat, 82, 83, 123, 164

schedule, 39, 51, 73, 98, 141, 144, 145, 156, 157
scheduling, 77
school, 2-4, 26, 31-33, 37, 39, 74, 88, 107, 141, 142, 146, 164

Sole Proprietor, 56, 98-100, 106, 126

spiritual, X, 7, 23-27, 29-31, 42, 48, 51, 154, 160

staff, 77, 145

student, 4, 6, 8, 14, 17, 20, 21, 27-29, 31, 32, 39-43, 46, 49-53, 55, 58-63, 71, 72, 74, 76, 83-88, 103, 105, 112, 113, 123, 124, 137, 141, 142, 152

substitute teachers, 3, 5

studio, X, 3, 5, 6, 8, 9, 12, 12, 16-18, 26-28, 33, 42, 45, 50, 58, 59, 66, 67, 70, 75, 77, 85-87, 90, 93, 102-104, 106, 109, 111-114, 116-118, 120, 121, 123-125, 129, 132, 133, 135-149, 157, 158, 163

teaching schedule, 39, 51, 156, 157

teaching, 2, 5-7, 9, 12-15, 17-21, 24-30, 32-34, 36-44, 48, 51, 52, 55, 60, 61, 66, 67, 82, 83, 87, 102, 110, 112, 123, 134-136, 143, 152, 153, 156, 157, 164

teacher training, IX, 2, 11-19, 21, 70, 117, 141, 147

vacation, 124, 133, 164

values, 59, 63

website, 71-76, 79, 80, 83-87, 91, 92, 94, 101, 103, 106, 108, 117, 121, 128

WordPress, 73-75, 79, 83, 84

workshops, 66, 73, 77, 79, 144

Yoga Alliance, 16, 19, 121

Yoga Journal, 81

Yoga Sutras of Patanjali, 15, 19

yoga teachers, X, 4, 7, 9, 13, 15-18, 23, 31, 43, 49, 50, 57, 58, 73, 102-104, 108, 140, 142-145, 147, 156, 164

Made in the USA
Monee, IL
28 February 2020